BASEBALL AND SOFTBALL

The Skills of the Game

THE • SKILLS • OF • THE • GAME

BASEBALL
AND SOFTBALL

Ian Smyth

The Crowood Press

First Published in 1995 by
The Crowood Press Ltd
Ramsbury, Marlborough
Wiltshire SN8 2HR

British Library Cataloguing-in-Publication Data

A catalogue for this book is available from the British Library.

ISBN 1 85223 875 5

Picture credits
All photographs by Ian Smyth
Line-drawings by Annette Findlay

Throughout this book, he, him and his have been used as neutral pronouns and as such refer to both males and females.

Typeset and designed by D & N Publishing, Ramsbury, Wiltshire.

Phototypeset by FIDO Imagesetting, Witney, Oxon.

Printed and bound by The Bath Press.

Typefaces used: text, Univers 55; headings, Univers 65 and Plantin.

Contents

Having spent my baseball years either as an opposing team manager or on various committees alongside Ian Smyth, I respect his views as a fellow devotee of our game, and admire his practical approach to coaching the way it should be played.

This manual will instruct and entertain you as you learn the fundamentals, and enlighten you as you grow into a seasoned player or coach. Baseball is rich in tradition and hopefully you will become part of that family and history. This guide by Ian will start you on the way to your first hit and to that grand slam.

Steve Herbert
President, British Baseball Federation

For years baseball has suffered from insufficient opportunities to involve teachers and students in grass roots learning of the game. While many books have been written about the fundamentals of baseball, too many are out-dated and not conversant with the more up-to-date techniques.

Ian Smyth provides in this book an opportunity for aficionados of baseball to learn its finer points from one of Britain's most forward-thinking baseball coaches. Ian has had a wealth of experience at all levels, from local clubs to international teams. Here Ian shares the results of that experience, along with techniques and theories, in a way that will make any player a better player, and any coach a better coach.

Ralph Rago
Envoy Coach, Major League
Baseball International

Ian Smyth BA (Hons), MA, was trained at Carnegie School of Physical Education in Leeds. He has been involved with baseball at all levels, in both coaching and administration, and, as well as being coach with the Great Britain national baseball squad, he is at present the Director of Coaching for the British Baseball Federation, concentrating on the Federation's Coach Education Programmes.

1

History and Development

The actual origins of the game of baseball are shrouded in controversy and doubt. Striking games have been noted throughout history from the ancient Egyptians onwards, via many different civilizations and cultures. Similarities between the English game of rounders and baseball have fuelled this debate. Some argue that the Pilgrim Fathers took the game to America. Nevertheless, the game of baseball as we know it is a product of the United States. Although there are many similar games played all over the world, the origins of organized baseball can be traced back to nineteenth-century America.

The modern game of baseball has developed from the 'Cartwright Rules', which were established in 1846. Cartwright, a surveyor, formed the rules, which included formal guidelines and playing rules. He umpired the first game played under these rules between the Knickerbockers and the New York Nine at Elysian Fields, Hoboken, New Jersey on 19 June, 1846. The New Yorkers won comfortably 23–1.

Over the next quarter of a century, baseball spread throughout the United States. Clubs were established all over the country, forming a huge amateur following. This remained the case until 1869, when businessmen in Cincinnati,

Ohio, formed a professional baseball club, which would bring pride and prestige to the city. Ironically the man put in charge of the club was an Englishman, Harry Wright, who was from Sheffield.

Wright was paid $1,200 to manage the team and play centre field. The Cincinnati Red Stockings, as they were known, then proceeded on a barn-storming tour of the United States, covering over 11,000 miles, and compiling a record of fifty-six wins and one tie.

Despite the fact that the Red Stockings played against amateur teams, their tour and organization paved the way for a professional baseball league. The development of this league came in 1871, with the formation of the National Association of Professional Base-Ball Players. Nine clubs paid the $10 entry fee, and became charter members. They included the Boston Red Stockings, Chicago White Stockings, Cleveland Forest Citys, Fort Wayne Kekiongas, New York Mutuals, Philadelphia Athletics, Rockford Forest Citys, Washington Nationals and the Washington Olympics. James Kerns of Philadelphia was elected League President.

In 1871 the Philadelphia Athletics won the championship with a record of twenty-two wins and seven losses. Chicago finished second, with Boston in third place. Then from 1872 to 1875, Boston dominated the league, winning the championship every season. Unfortunately, this domination was partly responsible for the demise of the league. Boston's dominance, along with alleged bribery, gambling and corruption, led to a loss of public confidence in baseball, which was reflected in decreasing attendances.

However, William Hulbert, who owned the Chicago club, resurrected the game by forming the National League of Professional Baseball Clubs in 1876 (and this league still exists today). Hulbert ran this league until his death in 1882, steering it through scandals, crises and franchise movements.

In 1880 another major league was formed, mainly through the actions of the Cincinnati club. Prior to this, Cincinnati were expelled from the National League for playing on Sundays and for allowing the sale of alcohol at their ground. They therefore founded the American Association. Initially the National League refused to recognize the American Association, which led to a fierce battle for players and spectators. The American Association scheduled games on Sundays, and reduced admission prices by 50 per cent. This gave them the slight edge in terms of attracting spectators.

The National League realized that the bickering between the two leagues was bad for business. Therefore, in 1883, the National League president, A.G. Mills, brought about the National Agreement between the two leagues. This lasted until 1891, when the American Association withdrew in a dispute over players. Regrettably for the American Association this caused the demise of their league.

This left the National League in total control of Major League baseball for the next decade. Then in 1901, Byron 'Ban' Johnson established the American League. Despite initial problems with the rival National League, they reached an agreement to control organized baseball. To mark this, a play-off between the winners of the respective leagues was organized. This became known as the World Series, with the inaugural winners being the Boston Red Sox.

Over the next thirty years, baseball's popularity fluctuated. In 1919 it reached crisis point when the World Series between the Chicago White Sox and the Cincinnati Reds was thrown by the White Sox in a betting fix. This became known as the Black Sox scandal. Baseball was on the verge of disaster. However, all the club owners appointed a lawyer, Kenesaw Mountain Landis, as the first commissioner of baseball. His first action was to ban the Black Sox for life. Landis ruled with an iron fist, and worked tirelessly to increase the popularity of professional baseball.

At the time of the Black Sox scandal, the greatest ever player hit the major leagues. In 1919, Babe Ruth broke the home run record while playing for the Boston Red Sox. The next season he was sold to the New York Yankees, and subsequently hit fifty-four home runs in one season. The increase in the number of home runs, assisted by a livelier ball, started to bring the crowds back to baseball.

During the depression of the 1930s baseball provided the chance for people to forget about the economic problems of the time. Attendances increased dramatically, and in 1935 in Cincinnati the first night game was held. The advent of night games enabled people to go to the ball games after work.

The 1930s also witnessed the first live radio broadcast of games. Initial fears were that live broadcasts would reduce attendances, but the opposite proved to be true, and attendances actually increased. The popularity of baseball was such that during the Second World War the Major Leagues continued to play for the 'morale of the country'. This was decreed by President Eisenhower. After the Second World War, baseball experienced massive changes, many of which reflected change in society generally. Nevertheless, baseball was never to be the same again. In 1947 Jackie Robinson became the first black player to play in the major leagues when he was bought in by Branch Rickey, the owner of the Brooklyn Dodgers. Despite resentment and harassment, Robinson won the Rookie of the Year Award in his first season, and had a distinguished career. He forged the way for other black and Latin players to follow his example.

In the post-war period, communications improved rapidly. Two innovations shaped the future of baseball – commercial air travel and television.

Television had taken over from radio as the main medium for broadcasting baseball. More and more people were seeing Major League baseball for the first time, and again its popularity increased. The development of commercial air travel also had a profound effect on the game. Before this, Major League baseball was restricted to the cities of the East Coast and the Mid-West. However, air travel changed the face of the game forever.

In 1953, the Boston Braves moved to Milwaukee. Five years later, the New York Giants and the Brooklyn Dodgers moved to San Francisco and Los Angeles respectively. This movement west led to a growth in the number of clubs. In 1961 the American League expanded to ten teams. The National League followed suit in 1962. Further growth came in 1969, with both leagues increasing to twelve teams. In 1977 the American League again expanded to fourteen teams. The National League eventually followed in 1993.

By 1994 Major League baseball had realigned to create three divisions within each league:

American League

East	Central	West
Boston Red Sox	Cleveland Indians	Oakland Athletics
New York Yankees	Chicago White Sox	Seattle Marines
Toronto Blue Jays	Kansas City Royals	Texas Rangers
Baltimore Orioles	Minnesota Twins	California Angels
Detroit Tigers	Milwaukee Brewers	

National League

East	Central	West
Atlanta Braves	St. Louis Cardinals	San Francisco Giants
Montreal Expos	Houston Astros	Los Angeles Dodgers
Philadelphia Phillies	Chicago Cubs	Colorado Rockies
New York Mets	Cincinnati Reds	San Diego Padres
Florida Marlins	Pittsburgh Pirates	

This realignment has altered the structure of the end of season play-offs. At the end of the regular season of 162 games, the three divisional winners and the runner-up with the best record will go to the play-offs. The winners of these play-offs will meet the winners of the National League in the World Series, which is played over the best of seven games. The World Series champions in 1994 were the Toronto Blue Jays. In 1992 they became the first team from outside the United States to win the World Series and in 1993 they retained the title by defeating the Philadelphia Phillies. The top stars in the Major Leagues stand to make a great deal of money. In 1993, Barry Bonds, of the San Francisco Giants, signed a six-year contract worth $44 million!

INTERNATIONAL BASEBALL

As well as in the United States, baseball is also played in many countries world-wide. In Japan, baseball is the number one sport, with the Tokyo Yorimuri Giants being the biggest club. The Japanese have had professional baseball since the end of the Second World War.

Elsewhere professional baseball exists in the Caribbean and Central America. Puerto Rico, the Dominican Republic, Venezuela and Mexico have strong professional leagues. On an amateur basis, Cuba have dominated the world game for over twenty years and it is believed that the Cubans are possibly a match for the professional teams in the United States.

In Asia, there are professional leagues in Korea and Taiwan as well as Japan. The game has also spread to China, so the rest of the baseball world will have to be ready.

Australia now possesses a professional league supported by Major League baseball. There are currently over thirty Australians signed with Major League teams.

Europe, although not as strong as Asia and the Americas also has professional baseball. In Holland and Italy, semi-professional leagues are very successful, as are those in other European nations such as Spain, France and Sweden.

BASEBALL IN THE OLYMPICS

In 1992 in Barcelona, baseball became a full medal sport. Prior to this baseball had been a demonstration sport six times and the winners of the respective tournaments were:

1912	USA
1936	'WORLD AMATEURS'
1956	AMERICAN SERVICES TEAM
1964	USA
1984	JAPAN
1988	USA
1992	CUBA

For the 1996 games in Atlanta, the International Olympic Committee are hoping that the top professional players from the Major Leagues will participate. This should provide intriguing match-ups between USA, Japan and Cuba, the chief baseball-playing nations.

BASEBALL IN BRITAIN

Baseball in Britain has experienced a chequered past. Baseball has been played in this country since 1874, when a tour of American professionals was held.

The Baseball Association of Great Britain was founded in 1890. It appears that former Boston and Cincinnati player A.G. Spalding was the driving force behind this development. Spalding, a sports goods manufacturer, offered to finance baseball teams that were associated with any professional football club. However, only four clubs, Derby, Stoke, Preston and Aston Villa took up the offer. Aston Villa were the first champions, but this enterprise was short-lived.

The boom period for British baseball came in the 1930s. In 1933 Sir John Moores of Littlewoods Pools established the National Baseball Association. From 1935–9, he helped to develop leagues all over the country, including Lancashire, Yorkshire, London, Birmingham and South Wales. Many amateur leagues were formed, and from the period 1936–9, professional leagues were developed in both the north of England and the London area. The highlight of this period was the victory by England over the United States in a five-match series. This was acknowledged by the International Baseball Association as the first World Amateur Championships.

The onset of the Second World War restricted the growth of baseball in this country. However the game still remained strong in areas such as Hull, Liverpool, Nottingham and London. Presently the game in Britain is administered by the British Baseball Federation. The showpiece of the game is the National Premier League, which consists of fifteen teams in two divisions.

BBF National Premier League

North	South
Humberside Mets	Enfield Spartans
Leeds City Royals	Hounslow
Nottingham Hornets	Rangers
Liverpool Trojans	Brighton
Humberside	Buccaneers
Warriors	Crawley Comets
Birmingham Braves	Bristol Black Sox
Menwith Hill pirates	Essex Arrows
	London Warriors
	Hemel Red Sox

At the end of the regular season, the winners of the respective divisions participate in a three-game play-off to decide the national champions. In 1994 the Humberside Mets won the NPL series. The NPL is fed by regional leagues based throughout the country.

Great Britain also competes at international level, with senior (open age) and junior (age 16–18) teams. In 1988 Great Britain won the European B Championships held in Birmingham. In 1993 Great Britain juniors won the European B Championships in Barcelona.

SOFTBALL

The sport of softball is essentially a derivative of baseball, and can be traced back to 1887. At that time, George Hancock, of the Farragu Boat Club in Chicago, developed a game that could be played indoors during the harsh winter months. Legend has it that this idea developed from a makeshift game in which a tied-up boxing glove and a broom stick were used. The glove did not travel very far when hit, and therefore gave Hancock the idea for an indoor game. He further developed the game by establishing a code of rules and called the game indoor baseball.

The game became very popular during the winter months, but also became popular in its own right, and many people began playing the game outdoors during the summer. It subsequently became known as indoor-outdoor baseball.

However, Hancock did not have a monopoly on the development of such

11

games. Several versions, including kitten ball, mush ball and diamond ball, were popular in the northern towns and cities of the United States. Each city had its own variation of the game.

In 1926 the National Recreation Conference attempted to standardize the rules. It was at this conference that Walter Hakason of the Denver YMCA introduced the name of softball. Over the next five years this became the universal name for the sport, although many regional variations of the game still existed.

This problem came to a head in Milwaukee in 1932, when a cross-regional tournament was held. Confusion reigned as the thirty competing teams had at least a dozen different sets of rules between them. This prompted Leo Fischer to organize a conference, which would attempt to standardize the rules of softball. This was held at the Chicago World's Fair in 1933. As a result, the Amateur Softball Association was established to govern the sport in the United States.

The game of softball grew rapidly in the 1930s and 1940s. In 1950 the International Softball Federation was established. The first World Championships for women were held in 1965, and for men in 1966.

Softball has now become a world game. There are still different forms around, notably fast-pitch and slow-pitch. The game is played by both men and women in mixed or single-sex teams.

2
Introduction to the Game of Baseball

Baseball is played between two teams of nine players. The object of the game is to score more runs than the opposition. A run is scored when a batter advances around all the bases reaching home plate. A run can be scored in stages, in that the batter does not have to get all the way around on one hit. If the batter does get around on one hit, this is called a home run.

A baseball game consists of nine innings, with each team batting nine times. An innings ends when three players of the batting side are out. The batter is allowed three strikes before being called out; on the other hand, four balls allows the batter a 'walk' to first base.

A strike is a pitched ball that passes over the home plate between the batter's knees and armpits. This area is known as the strike zone. A strike will also be called if the batter swings and misses, whatever the location. If the batter hits the ball into foul territory, a strike will also be called, for the first two strikes. Strikes are called by the home plate umpire, who is positioned directly behind the catcher. A ball is called when a pitched ball is outside the strike zone, and the batter does not swing. A fair hit is a batted ball that settles in fair territory in the infield or lands in fair territory in the outfield. If a batted ball is caught on the fly by any fielder the batter is out.

A batter must run for first base once he hits the ball; he is out if the ball is held on first base before he reaches it. At second base, third base and home plate the runner must be actually tagged with the ball, unless the runners are forced to advance. No base can be occupied by more than one runner, therefore if there is a runner on first base and the batter hits the ball, the runner must run to second base to free first base for the batter. In this situation the fielder does not have to tag the runner: he can just step on the base with the ball in his possession. A base runner does not have to advance to the next base on a hit unless he is forced to by the next runner advancing.

DEFENSIVE POSITIONS
(Fig 1)

On defence the nine players are usually situated in the following positions:

1   Pitcher
2   Catcher
3   First base
4   Second base
5   Third base
6   Shortstop
7   Left field
8   Centre field
9   Right field

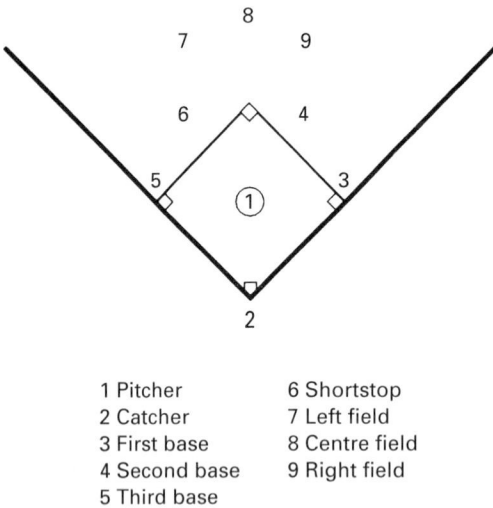

1 Pitcher
2 Catcher
3 First base
4 Second base
5 Third base

6 Shortstop
7 Left field
8 Centre field
9 Right field

Fig 1   The standard defensive positions.

The essence of the game of baseball is the duel between pitcher and batter. The pitcher has to outwit the batter using different pitches, speeds and target locations in the strike zone. The batter's job is to get on base safely, then to attempt to score. Generally the pitcher has the upper hand, with even the best batters only getting fair hits in three out of ten attempts.

PLAYING AREA
(Fig 2)

The baseball field is formed by two lines (foul lines) that run from home plate through first and third base, creating a 90 degree arc. The inner part of this segment is the infield, the outer part is called the outfield.

The infield is formed by a 90ft (27.5m) 'diamond', which has a base on each corner. Each of these bases must be touched by the runner to score a run.

The outfield is formed by the two foul lines, which should extend at least 250ft (76m) to reach the outfield fence. The area between the foul lines is called fair territory. The areas outside the foul lines are called foul territory.

Pitcher's mound
(Fig 3)

Within the infield there are two important areas. The first is the pitcher's mound, which is a raised area, where the pitcher delivers the ball from. The mound is elevated 10in (25cm) above the level of the home plate. It has a radius of 18ft (5.5m). On top of the mound is a pitcher's plate (also called a pitching rubber), which measures 24in x 6in (73cm x 18cm). The pitcher must be in contact with this plate when he starts his delivery.

Home Plate Area
(Fig 4)

The other important area of the infield is the home plate area. The centre of this area is the home plate itself, which is a five-sided piece of rubber, 17in (51cm) wide.

Either side of home plate is a batter's box, in one of which the batter must stand when hitting the ball. If the batter hits the ball while being out of this box, he will be called out.

Behind the home plate is a catcher's box, where the catcher fields the ball. The catcher must stay in this box until the pitcher has delivered the ball.

Fig 2   The playing area.

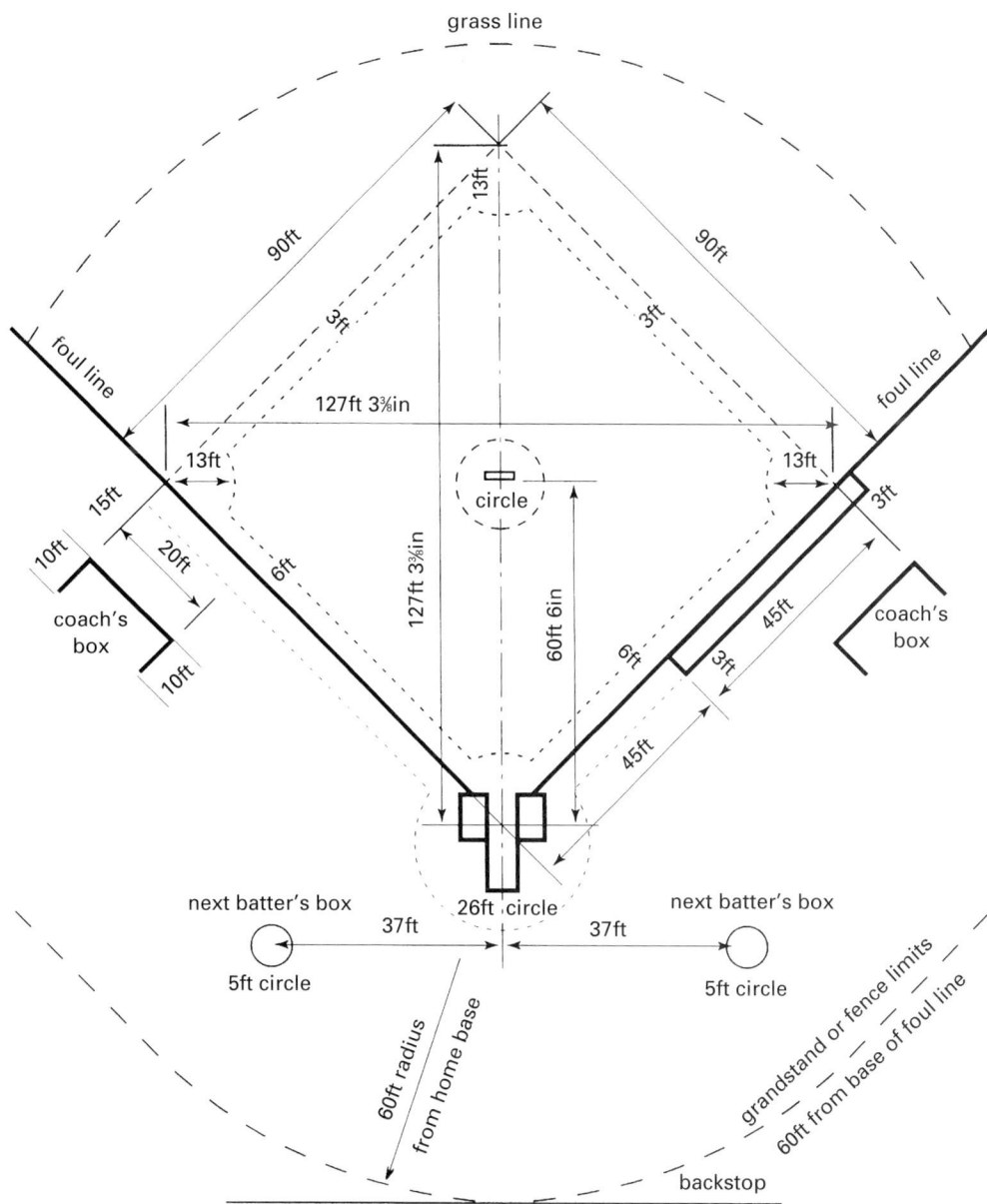

grass line

90ft

90ft

13ft

foul line

3ft

3ft

foul line

127ft 3⅜in

13ft

13ft

3ft

15ft

20ft

127ft 3⅜in

circle

60ft 6in

45ft

coach's box

10ft

6ft

6ft

3ft

coach's box

10ft

45ft

next batter's box

26ft circle

next batter's box

37ft

37ft

5ft circle

5ft circle

60ft radius from home base

grandstand or fence limits

60ft from base of foul line

backstop

15

Fig 3   The pitching mound.

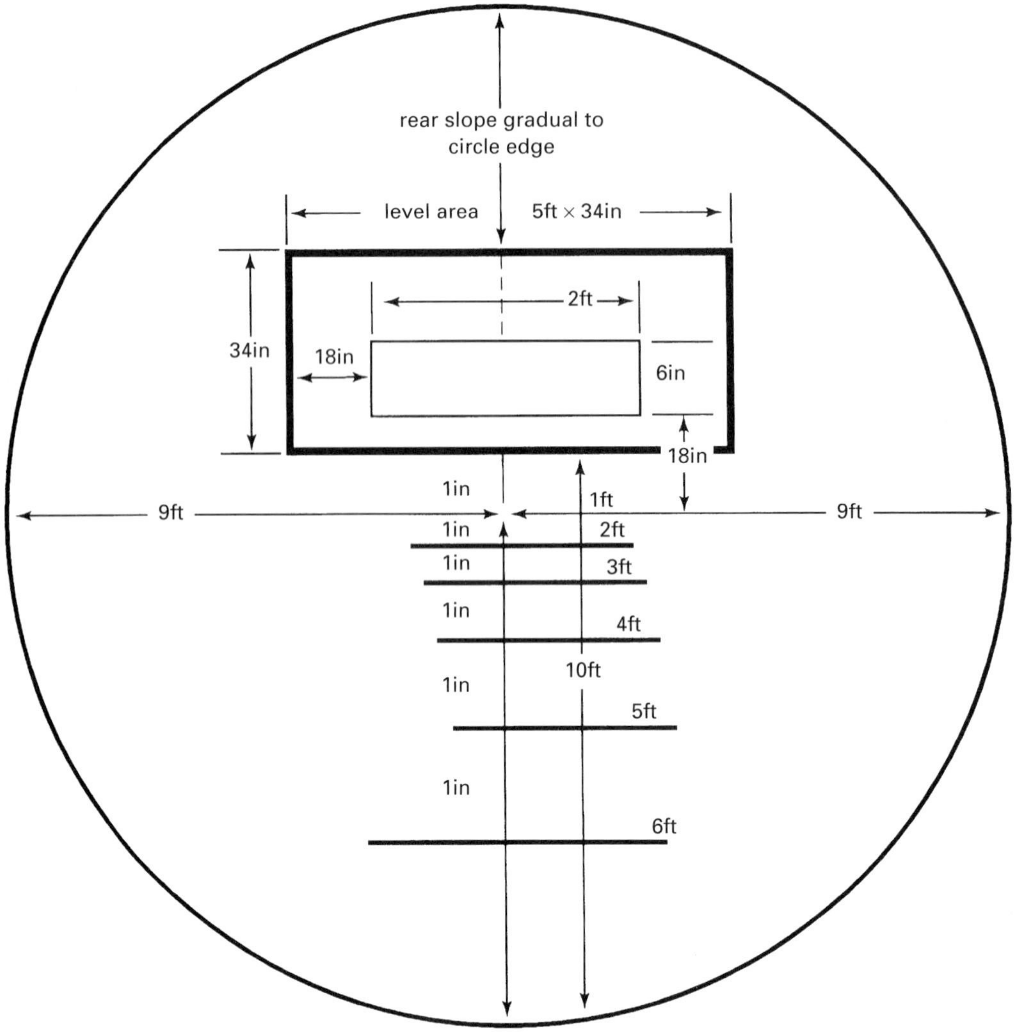

rear slope gradual to
circle edge

level area   5ft × 34in

34in   18in   2ft

6in

1in   1ft
9ft   2ft   9ft
1in   3ft
1in   4ft
1in   10ft
1in   5ft
1in   6ft

18in

Fig 4 The home plate area.

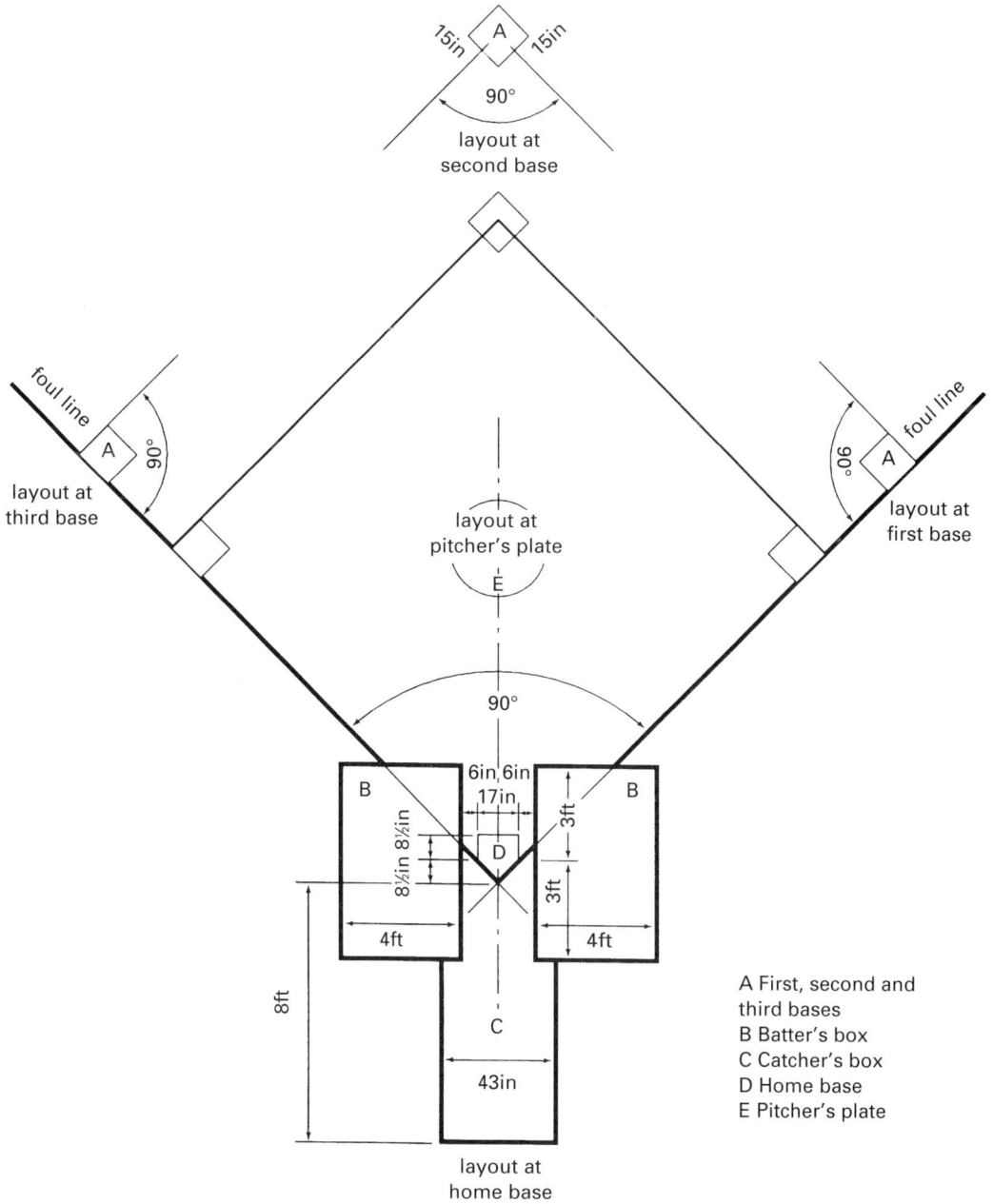

A First, second and third bases
B Batter's box
C Catcher's box
D Home base
E Pitcher's plate

17

EQUIPMENT
(Fig 5)

Playing Equipment

Baseball is essentially a bat and ball game. Therefore the two main pieces of equipment are the bat and ball. Other items, such as gloves, protective equipment and field equipment are still necessary, however, for an organized game.

BATS
The rules of baseball state that a bat must be a smooth rounded stick with a maximum diameter of 2¾in (8.5cm), and a maximum length of 42in (128cm).

In Major League baseball in America professionals are only allowed to use wooden bats, and these are generally made of ash. Most amateurs will use aluminium bats, which are much more durable. They will last much longer than wooden bats, and so will be less expensive in the long run. Most players will use bats that weigh between 28oz and 34oz (790–964g). Babe Ruth used a bat that weighed 54oz (1.5kg).

Beginners will probably try to use the biggest bat available. They will be under the incorrect impression that this will enable them to hit the ball harder and further. Insist instead that beginners use a light bat, which will be easier to control and therefore easier to hit the ball with.

BALL
The ball is made from white leather bound around a core of cork. It is round and has a circumference of 9–9¼in (24cm). It weighs 5–5¼oz (140g). The ball is stitched together in such a way that two raised seams are formed. These

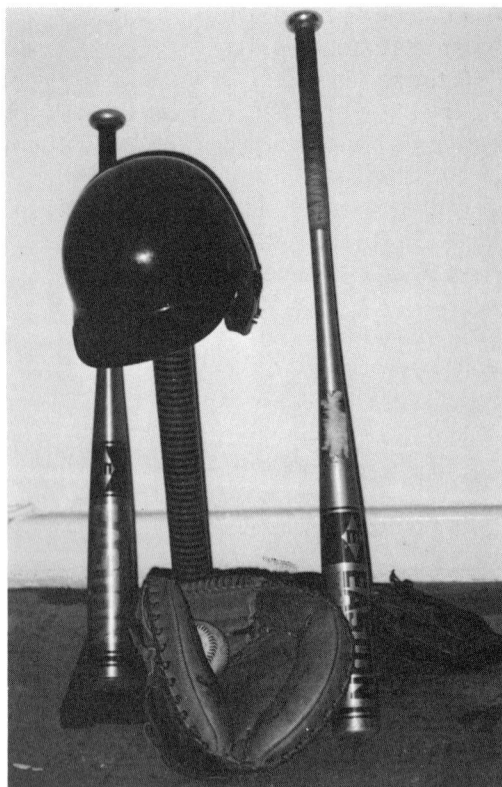

Fig 5   Playing equipment.

seams are used by the pitcher to make the ball move in a particular way when he pitches. Traditionally baseballs were made in Cuba and Haiti, but now most are made in the Far East.

GLOVES
All of the fielders wear gloves while they are fielding. The gloves are made of leather, but are lightweight and have a pocket (or webbing), which allows the fielder to catch the ball more easily.

There are three main kinds of glove. The catcher wears a specialized catcher's mitt, which has lots of padding to protect

18

the catcher's hand. During the course of a game a catcher will receive the ball over 150 times, at speeds over 90 miles per hour (144kph). The mitt will protect the catcher's hand from damage under these circumstances.

The first baseman also has a special glove, which is a little bigger than a standard fielder's glove.

Infielders and outfielders will wear similar gloves. Generally the infielders will have smaller gloves, to enable a quick transfer of the ball from the glove to the throwing hand. Plays in the infield have to be executed quickly; the smaller size of the infielder's glove helps to facilitate faster play.

PROTECTIVE EQUIPMENT

In baseball it is now mandatory for all batters to wear batting helmets. These are plastic with foam padding, which protects the batter from head injuries which may be caused by a thrown or batted ball while either batting or base running.

CATCHER'S EQUIPMENT

Owing to the nature of the position, the catcher needs to be well protected. He has to wear a helmet, a face mask, throat protector, chest protector, cup and leg guards. This equipment is known as the 'tools of ignorance'.

Modern catching equipment is lightweight and user friendly. It provides adequate protection while allowing the catcher freedom of movement.

CAPS

The wearing of caps with a logo or letter on the front is traditional in baseball. Every self-respecting ball player or fan will have at least one baseball cap.

Field Equipment

HOME PLATE

Home plate is a five-sided piece of rubber, 17in (43cm) wide and 17in (43cm) long. It needs to be secured to the ground so that it does not move during the course of the game.

PITCHER'S PLATE

The pitcher's plate is also made out of rubber and is secured into the pitching mound 10in (25cm) above the level of home plate, 60½ft (18.5m)away.

BASES

The three bases are square pieces of white canvas 15in x 15in (38 x 38cm) filled with foam. These are also secured to the ground, and are situated at the corners of the diamond.

BACKSTOP

Most baseball fields will have some form of backstop. This will prevent the ball from flying straight back behind the batter into the crowd. The backstop should be at least 60ft (18m) behind the home plate. The height and width of the backstop varies, but it should be big enough to offer protection to spectators, and actually to stop the ball.

THROWING AND RECEIVING

Throwing

Throwing and catching are the primary skills that are needed to play both baseball and softball. Before any of the more advanced skills and drills can ever be attempted, throwing and catching must be mastered.

GRIP

The ball should always be gripped across four seams, as this will give a true, straight throw and the ball will not deviate in flight.

The middle and index fingers are placed on top of the ball, slightly apart. The thumb is placed directly under the ball, making it sit comfortably in the fingers. It is important at this stage not to let the ball rest too far back in the hand, as we want it to be thrown with the fingers. When the ball is released, it comes off the ends of the index and middle fingers, creating backspin.

ARM MOVEMENT
(Figs 6–8)
Ideally the arm should be over the top of the ball in the throwing motion. This will reduce the stress on the shoulder joint, and create an efficient throwing action.

Fig 7   The throwing sequence (1): the arm points downwards.

Before the throw the glove side should be turned towards the target. This will put the thrower in a side-on position. The arm should be drawn downwards and backwards, imitating a circular movement. As the movement of the arm comes forwards, the elbow goes past the head, followed by the forearm and the wrist. At this point of the forward motion, the thrower starts to stride towards the target.

STRIDE
(Fig 9)
As the thrower starts to stride, the hips should turn, opening the body towards

Fig 6   The side-on position for throwing.

20

Fig 8   The throwing sequence (2): the arm goes back.

Fig 9   The throwing sequence (3): the arm is up ready to release the ball.

the target. The weight is shifted from the rear to the front foot. The thrower then pushes off the rear foot, creating momentum towards the target. As the weight transfers over the front foot, the arm comes forwards and releases the ball.

FOLLOW THROUGH
(Fig 10)
As the ball is released the thrower should follow through, bending forwards at the waist. The throwing arm swings across the body. The thrower should imagine that he is throwing his shoulder into the receiver's glove.

Fig 10   The throwing sequence (4): the follow through.

Drills
The best drill for throwing and catching is simply to play catch. In pairs, players should throw to each other concentrating on proper throwing and receiving technique.

To emphasize the mechanics, players should play catch from their knees, progressing to one knee, then to standing. This will isolate the arm, allowing the coach to concentrate on proper techniques. Gradually introduce progressions of turning, stepping and throwing.

Fig 11   Receiving the ball above the waist.

Fig 12   Receiving the ball below the waist.

Receiving
(Figs 11 & 12)

The receiver should have his feet shoulder width apart, with the throwing-side foot slightly behind. The knees should be bent so the receiver stands in a comfortable position. This will enable movement to either side if there is a bad throw.

The receiver concentrates on the flight of the ball, watching the ball at all times with the palm of the glove facing it.

The receiver catches the ball with two hands. On receiving the ball he should absorb its speed by flexing his hands and elbows, thereby cushioning the ball into the glove.

RECEIVING ABOVE THE WAIST
The ball should be caught in the centre of the body. If the ball is above the waist, the hands should be at chest level with the thumbs together. If the ball is below the waist the glove should be held palm upwards, with the little fingers together. As the ball is caught it should be brought into the waist.

3
Pitching

The pitcher is the most important player in the baseball team. Any successful baseball team will have good pitchers. A pitcher needs to have a strong, accurate throwing arm. Moreover, successful pitchers have the ability to throw different kinds of pitches, to deceive the batter. These different types of pitches are discussed below.

Good pitchers need to be fit and strong. Most will throw between 100 and 150 pitches each game, so they need to have strong legs, shoulders and backs to cope with the level of stress involved. Young pitchers should only throw around sixty pitches a game to prevent the risk of injury.

PITCHING PHASES

Pitching as a skill can be broken down into six phases:

1   Grip
2   Wind up
3   Pivot
4   Stride
5   Release
6   Follow through

Grip

Baseball pitchers have over the years developed a vast array of pitches which are intended to deceive the batter. Many pitchers have developed their own variations of pitches, but there are six standard pitches. For a pitcher to be successful he needs to be able to master at least two, and preferably three, different pitches.

FASTBALL
(Figs 13–15)
Practically all pitchers will have a fastball in their armoury. Hard-throwing pitchers can intimidate even accomplished batters with a good fastball.

There are two main grips for the fastball. For the four-seam fastball the fingers grip the ball across the seams, so that it is held with the first two fingers on the top of the ball and the thumb underneath. This pitch will give the ball a true line to the catcher with little or no deviation.

By gripping the ball along the seams, the pitcher will throw a two-seam fastball. This pitch should deviate a little more than a four-seam fastball, because of the wind resistance against the seams. This deviation of the path of the ball will hopefully fool the batter.

The intention of the fastball is to beat the batter with pure pace. However, even the fastest pitchers will get hit if they are unable to throw another type of pitch as the batter will eventually learn to cope with it. Therefore it is vital to have at least one more pitch if the pitcher is to be effective and unpredictable.

Fig 13   The four-seam fastball.

Fig 14   The two-seam fastball.

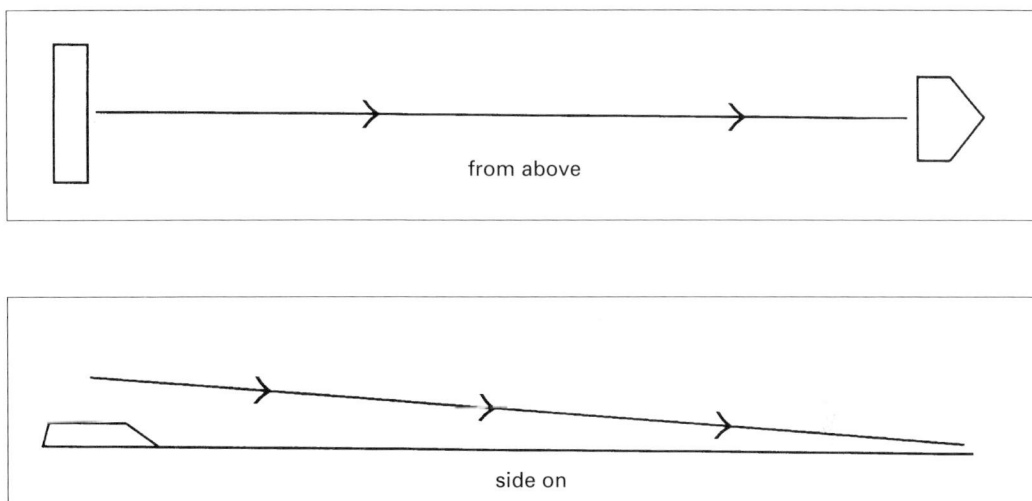

Fig 15   The flight of the fastball.

CURVEBALL
(Figs 16 & 17)
The curveball is, as the name suggests, a ball that curves through the air. The intention of the curveball is to beat the batter with movement rather than speed. The ball is gripped parallel to the seams. When it is released the pitcher will snap his wrist, imparting spin on the ball, which enables the ball to break down-wards and sideways. A right-handed pitcher will make the ball break from right to left, a left-hander will move the ball from left to right.

SLIDER
(Figs 18 & 19)
The slider is essentially a cross between a curveball and a fastball. The grip is tighter than for a curveball, with the fingers slightly closer together. The slider is thrown harder than a curveball, which

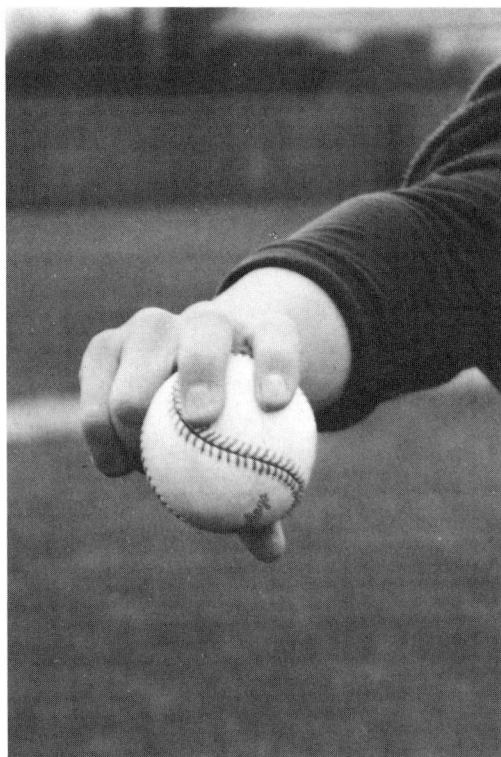

Fig 16   The curveball.

25

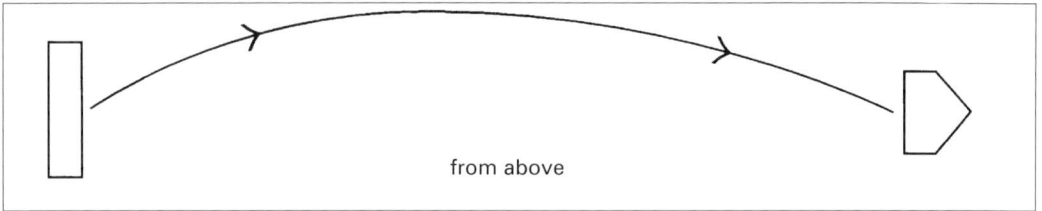

from above

Fig 17   The flight of the curveball.

Fig 18   The slider.

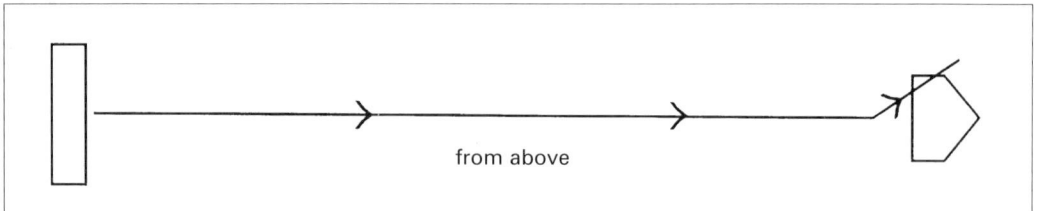

from above

Fig 19   The flight of the slider.

makes it similar to a fastball. Because of the speed of the slider, it will break less then a curveball, and later in its flight. Batters will think it is a fastball and will then be deceived by the last-minute break of the ball over home plate.

CHANGE UP
(Figs 20–22)
The change up is a pitch that aims to deceive the batter in its slower path to the plate. The purpose of the pitch is to fool the batter, so the pitcher must attempt to make the delivery look exactly the same as a fastball. The pitcher's movements, arm speed and release should be the same as for a fastball, giving the batter

Target Drill
Objectives Encourage pitchers to hit specific spots.
Equipment Balls, strike zone taped to a wall or fence.
Drill Pitcher pitches to specific spots in the strike zone: middle, high inside, low inside, high outside, low outside. He should start at 30ft (9m) and gradually move back to 60½ft (18.5m).
Coaching points Insist on correct mechanics. Record balls and strikes. Only allow sixty to seventy throws from full distance.
Can throw against imaginary batters.

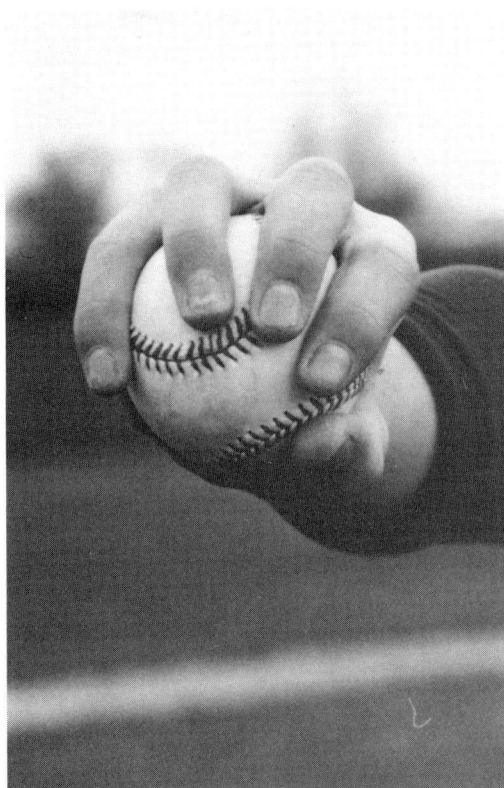

Fig 20   The palm ball.

Fig 21   The OK change up.

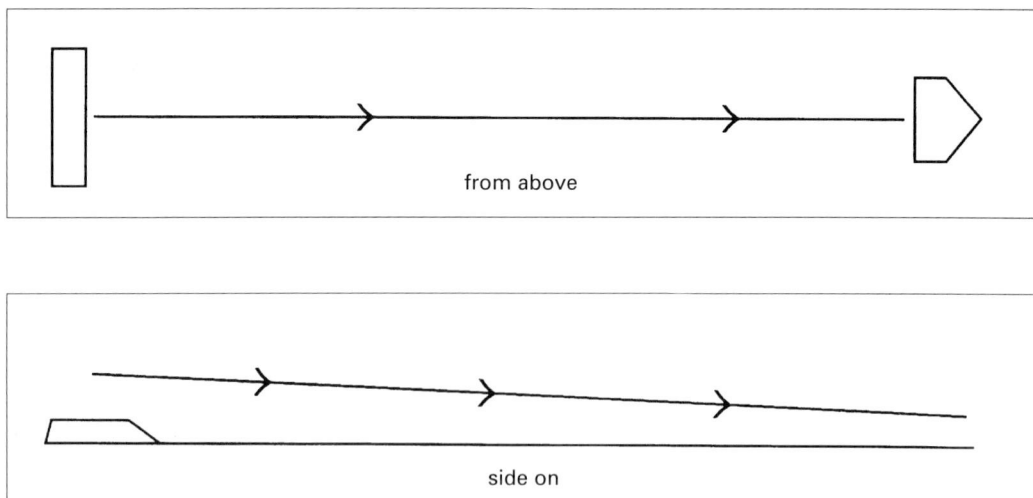

Fig 22   The flight of the change up.

absolutely no cues. The grip on the ball will make it travel more slowly to the plate, however, and as the batter will hopefully be expecting a fastball, he will swing too early.

The grip for the change up varies from pitcher to pitcher. The two most popular grips are the palm ball, where the ball is pushed back into the palm of the pitching hand, and the OK change up, where the thumb and forefinger make a circle for the ball to rest in.

FORKBALL/SPLIT-FINGERED FASTBALL
(Figs 23 & 24)
As the name suggests, this pitch is a variation on a fastball. The difference is that for the forkball the fingers are spread wide, the ball resting between the index and second finger.

The delivery is the same as a fastball: the ball will travel directly towards the plate, but will break sharply downwards just before it reaches it. The batter will see a fastball all the way, then will be deceived by the last-minute break of the ball. If mastered, this pitch can be devastating.

Batting Practice
Objectives Make pitchers throw strikes.
Equipment Balls, bats, normal field equipment, pitching screen.
Drill Pitcher throws batting practice to rest of the team from behind a protective screen.
Can throw from the mound or a flat surface.
Coaching points Concentrate on throwing strikes.
Work on mechanics.

Fig 23   The split-fingered fastball.

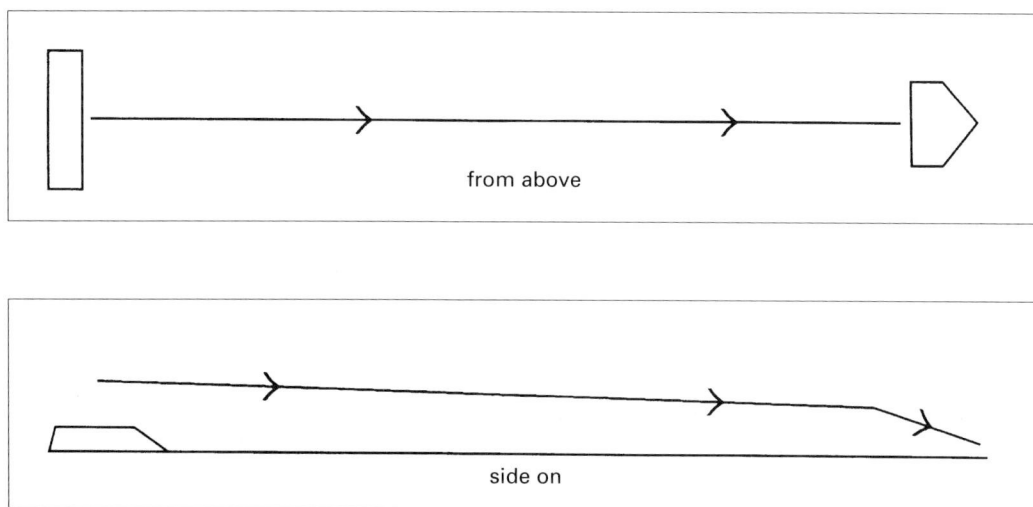

from above

side on

Fig 24   The flight of the split-fingered fastball (forkball).

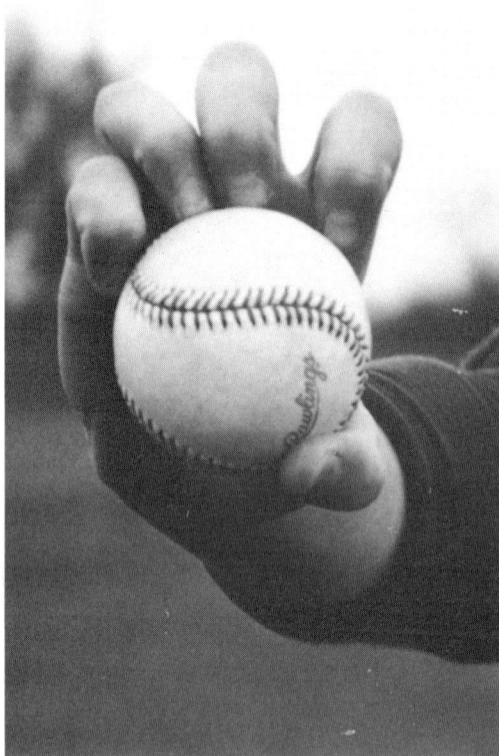

Fig 25 The knuckleball.

KNUCKLEBALL
(Fig 25)

The knuckleball is held between the thumb and knuckles of two or three fingers. This grip ensures the ball will not spin in flight, but will move because of air resistance on the seams of the ball.

This pitch works best in hot, humid conditions. The movement of the ball is unpredictable; not even the pitcher and catcher know what the ball will do. If the knuckleball is thrown too hard, it will flatten out, not move in the air, and be easy to hit.

This is a very difficult pitch to master, but it is very effective if thrown properly.

Wind Up
(Fig 26)

Once the pitcher has come to a decision about which pitch to select, he has then to throw it. The pitching motion begins with the wind up.

The pitcher will start facing the batter, concentrating on the catcher's mitt. To start the wind up, the pitcher will step back with his non-throwing-side foot (that is, the left foot for a right-handed pitcher, vice versa for a left-hander) and raise his arms. All through this phase the ball should be concealed from the batter, to avoid giving away any clues about the pitch.

This phase will provide the momentum for the rest of the pitching sequence.

Fig 26 The wind up (1): step back.

Fig 27　The wind up (2): pivot phase.

Fig 28　The wind up (3): stride phase.

Fig 29　The wind up (3): stride phase (side-on view).

Pivot
(Fig 27)

The pivot is the key part of the pitching motion, and requires good balance. The right-handed pitcher will pivot on the right foot, so that it turns parallel to the pitching plate, but remains in contact with it. He then shifts the weight on to the pivot foot raising the left leg into the air. The left-hander will pivot on his left foot.

Stride
(Figs 28 & 29)

Once the pitcher is in the pivot position, he needs to drive forward with his drive leg (right leg if he is right-handed, left leg for left-handers).

31

During the stride the left foot will be pointed towards third base for a right-hander. For left-handed pitchers, the right foot will be pointing towards first base. Just before the foot lands, it turns towards home plate. This opening of the foot will enable the hips to open, and bring the upper body through.

When the front foot lands the knee will bend slightly to absorb the impact. The weight will move over this front knee, bringing the body into position to release the ball.

Release

Once the weight is over the front knee, the body is in the optimal position for the pitch. The arm will move forward, keeping the elbow high, and the ball is released towards home plate, with the necessary spin for the pitch selected.

Follow Through
(Fig 30)

The follow through is vital for speed, control and correct fielding position.

After releasing the ball the arm snaps across the body and the pivot foot should swing around, so that the pitcher stands square to home plate. The pitcher is now a fielder and needs to be ready for any balls hit back towards the mound.

SET POSITION
(Fig 31)

If there are runners on base, the pitcher will have to adjust and pitch from the set position. If he pitches from a full wind up, the runners will have plenty of time to steal bases. Therefore the pitcher will

Fig 30   The wind up (4): the follow through.

Game Situation Drill
Objectives To allow pitcher to pitch in game-like conditions.
Equipment All normal game equipment.
Drill Pitcher pitches to the batting line-up. He can pitch a specific number of balls at bats, or a maximum number of pitches.
Coaching points Work the strike zone. Change speeds. Work on fielding positions after hits.

must come to a set position, where there must be a discernible stop. The ball can then be delivered to the plate, using the stride, release and follow through stages of the pitching motion.

PITCH LOCATION

Good pitchers will tend to keep the ball low in the strike zone. This has two main advantages. First, lower balls are generally more difficult to hit, and secondly if they are hit, they are more likely to be hit on the ground. This will then give the infielders the opportunity to make a play.

Pitchers should try to use the whole width of the plate by pitching at times both on the inside and outside parts of the plate. This will make the batters think more about the pitch, keeping them guessing.

It is vital for the pitchers to throw strikes. Nothing is more depressing for a pitcher and his team than walking batters. Pitchers should attempt to get ahead in the count by throwing the first pitch as a strike. This gives the pitcher the advantage, and puts the batter under greater pressure.

Another sign of a good pitcher is that he will change speeds. This keeps the batter off balance, not knowing what kind of pitch will come next. If a pitcher only has a fastball in his repertoire, the batters will be ready for it, and no matter how fast the pitch is, sooner or later the batters will catch up and hit the ball.

Fig 31   The set position.

have to deliver the ball more quickly to the plate to reduce the base stealing threat of the runners. This is where the set position comes in.

The pitcher stands sideways to the batter, placing the drive foot against the pitcher's plate. From this position, he

4
Catching

Catcher is probably the most demanding position in baseball. The catcher has to crouch behind home plate to receive pitches. He has to call the pitches through a series of signals with the pitcher. He is the leader on the field, as his position gives a view of the whole field: he can position players for specific plays. He must be strong, quick, agile, have good concentration and have a strong throwing arm.

Catchers must be alert to any offensive plays of the opposition, and must remember each batter, knowing their strengths, weaknesses and tendencies. He can then call for the pitch most likely to defeat any particular batter.

The catcher needs to wear a lot of protective equipment, including a helmet, face mask, throat protector, chest protector, protective cup and leg guards. Even in practice it is important that catchers wear the correct equipment.

GIVING SIGNALS
(Figs 32–35)

The first job of the catcher is to call the pitch. This is done by a series of signals using the fingers. The catcher's hand should be against his crotch when giving the signals, so that the opposing coaches and players cannot see the signal and thus anticipate which pitch is being thrown.

If there is a runner on base the catcher will have to give several signals, most of which will be decoys. If the catcher gives only one signal, the runner on second base will be able to see the sign and relay this information to the batter. Obviously the pitcher and catcher will have decided beforehand which is the real sign.

Fig 32   The fastball.

Fig 33   The curveball.

Fig 34   The change up.

Fig 35 (*Left*)   A speciality pitch.

Framing Drill
Objectives To teach the catcher to frame the ball, keeping borderline pitches in the strike zone.
Equipment Full catching equipment, balls and home plate.
Drill Two players (preferably both catchers): player A in catching position behind the plate, player B stands 25ft (7.5m) away, and throws the ball. The catcher will catch the ball keeping both the ball and the mitt in the strike zone. After ten repetitions the players swap places.
Coaching Points Correct glove position.
Hold the pitch, do not let the glove move out of the strike zone.

Fig 36 The catcher's basic position.

THE CATCHER'S POSITION
(Fig 36)

With no runners on base the catcher should assume a comfortable crouching position in the catcher's box, about 2ft (60cm) behind home plate. The legs should be shoulder width apart, with the weight on the balls of the feet. This enables the catcher to move quickly to get to a bad pitch in either direction.

The catcher should remain low in this position. This helps in two ways. Firstly it will give the pitcher a lower target, as the pitcher will be concentrating on the catcher's mitt. A low position will also give the umpire a better view of the plate.

If the catcher blocks the umpire's view, it becomes more difficult for the umpire to call strikes as he cannot see what is going on. Therefore it is in the catcher's interest to stay low.

The mitt should be used as a target, so the catcher should make it as large as possible by opening the glove wide.

Runners on Base – the 'Up' Position
(Fig 37)

With runners on base, the catcher has to assume a different position, so that he can move quickly to throw out any attempted base stealers. This is known as the 'up' position.

Right-handed catchers should have their right foot slightly in front of the left;

Fig 37 The catcher's 'up' position.

Throwing Drill
Objectives Practice quick, accurate throws to all bases.
Equipment Full catching equipment, balls, gloves and bases.
Drill Three players: A is catcher, B is pitcher and C is a baseman. Player A in catching position, B throws the ball, A catches it and throws to C who is at first base. After ten throws, C moves to second and then to third base. After one complete round the players swap positions.
Coaching points Correct catching and throwing mechanics.
Baseman should give a good target.

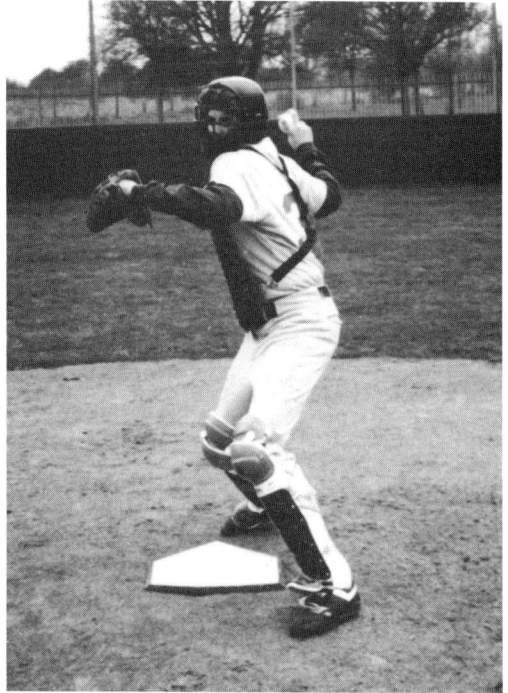

the reverse is true for left-handers. The back should be parallel to the ground, and as low as possible.

THROWING OUT BASE RUNNERS
(Figs 38 & 39)
If a runner attempts to steal second base the catcher should catch the ball while moving forwards, stepping towards second base with the back foot, while simultaneously rotating the shoulders parallel to the batter's box. The catcher should transfer the ball from the mitt to the throwing hand as quickly as possible, then make the throw by transferring his weight to the front foot, again rotating the shoulders and following through with the throwing arm.

Fig 38 *(Above)* Throwing out base stealers (1): the catcher drives out from behind the plate.

Fig 39 *(Right)* Throwing out base stealers (2): the catcher releases the ball in front of the plate.

BLOCKING THE BALL

If a ball is pitched in the dirt, the catcher's job is to stop the ball. Rather than attempting to catch it, the catcher should try and block it keeping the ball in front of him.

Ball in Front
(Fig 40)

If the ball is thrown in the dirt directly in front of the catcher, he should drop on to both knees, put the mitt between his legs, drop his chin on to his chest (to protect the throat area), and slide into the ball to execute the block. It is important the catcher keeps the ball in front; if not, the base runners will probably advance while the catcher wastes time trying to retrieve the ball.

Ball to the Side
(Fig 41)

If the ball is pitched to one side, the catcher should step out with the leg nearest the ball, keeping the ball in the centre of the body. The other leg drags behind, and the mitt is placed between the legs.

PLAYS AT HOME PLATE

Plays at home plate really highlight the courage of a catcher. Often these result in collisions; however, if the catcher is wearing the correct protective equipment and uses the right technique, injuries should be avoided.

Unless the bases are loaded, all plays at home plate will be tag plays, where the

Fig 40   Blocking the ball in front.

Fig 41   Blocking the ball to the side.

Fig 42   The catcher's fielding position when the bases are loaded.

Fig 43   The catcher making the tag.

catcher actually has to tag the runner with the ball.

Bases Loaded
(Fig 42)

If the bases are loaded and the batter hits the ball to the infield, the catcher should act as a first baseman. He should quickly get out of the crouch, place his right foot on the corner of the plate, and hold the mitt towards the fielder, giving a big target. As the ball is caught the catcher should move away from the plate, either to initiate a double play or simply to avoid the runner coming from third base.

Tag Plays
(Figs 43 & 44)

Tag plays at home plate are usually very exciting. If the catcher has plenty of time, he should catch the ball, placing the throwing hand into the mitt to secure it. He should then move down the third

Blocking Drill
Objectives To teach catchers correct blocking technique.
Equipment Full catching equipment, balls and home plate.
Drill Two players: Player B throws the ball into the dirt in front, to the left, and to the right of the catcher. The catcher aims to block the ball back towards home plate.
Coaching points Should block the ball with stomach and chest.
Should block the ball back towards home plate.
Should not block with the hands.
Should not try to catch the ball.

Fig 44   The catcher spinning towards the infield to check runners.

base line towards the runner, and as the runner comes past, he should apply the tag with both hands, then immediately spin anticlockwise towards the infield. This enables the catcher to be ready for any other play that may occur, and avoid any potential collisions.

PLAYS AT THE PLATE
(Figs 45 & 46)
If play is closer to home plate the catcher has to prepare for a play at the plate.

First he places his foot on the corner of home plate, pointing it directly along the

third base line, towards third base. This will protect the knee if a collision takes place. Furthermore, if the runner can see part of the plate, he will usually slide to try to reach home safely. This is exactly what the catcher wants. When he receives the ball, the catcher will take a little jab step towards the runner, effectively blocking the plate from the runner. The catcher can then apply the tag with two hands, which puts the runner out.

If the runner does not slide, the catcher has to prepare for a collision. In preparation he should drop his chin to his chest. the mitt should be out in front of the body, with the throwing hand securing the ball, and then he waits for the impact. In this situation the catcher must hold on to the ball. If he does the runner is out. If the ball is dropped the runner will be safe, and a run will be scored.

CATCHING POP-UPS

A pop-up is where the batter hits the ball directly upwards. If this ball is between home plate and the backstop, it is the catcher's responsibility to field it.

Immediately the ball is popped up, the catcher should come out of the crouch and locate the ball. Then the catcher should move towards the ball throwing the mask in the opposite direction. This will prevent him from tripping over the mask while making the catch.

The catcher needs to remember that most pop-ups will drift back towards the

Fig 45 *(Above right)*   The catcher preparing to block the plate.

Fig 46 *(Right)*   The catcher blocking the plate and making the tag.

infield. It is important, therefore, that he lines the ball up with the middle of his forehead. This will allow for any last minute adjustments. The catcher should catch the ball with his back to the infield, to ensure that the ball drifts towards, rather than away from him. The ball should be caught over the head with two hands.

If there are any runners on base, the catcher should pivot towards the infield immediately after catching the ball. If runners try to advance, the catcher is now in a good position to throw them out.

5
Infield

Four positions comprise the infield: first base, second base, third base and shortstop. As a unit they have to field every ground ball and make strong, accurate throws to the appropriate base to retire base runners.

Because of the nature of the game, it is very difficult for left-handed players to play any position in the infield except for first base. This is because a left-hander would have to shift his body through 180 degrees to make the throw, which would take far too long, giving the runners an advantage.

READY POSITION
(Fig 47)

All infielders should be in the ready position as the pitcher begins his motion.

The feet should be slightly more than shoulder width apart, knees should be bent, with the weight on the balls of the feet. The weight should be evenly distributed so that the player can move quickly in any direction where the ball is hit. The hand should be held low, in front of the body with the glove open.

FIELDING THE BALL

When the ball is hit the infielders should move into position so that the ball can be fielded.

It is important that the infielder stays low, because this will make it easier for him to adjust to any bad bounces of the ball. It is much easier to field a ball that

Fig 47   The infielder's ready position.

bounces up than to field a ball from an upright position if the ball stays low. The infielder also has to judge the speed, angle and spin on the ball, so that he can get into the right position to field the ball as quickly as possible.

Once in position, the infielder should keep his eye on the ball at all times. Both hands should be out in front of the body ready to collect the ball.

On catching the ball the infielder should field it into the glove, and trap it with the throwing hand. Using two hands has two advantages: the ball is in the throwing hand ready to throw, and fielding the ball with two hands will encourage the player to field it in the middle of the body.

While trapping the ball, the infielder should simultaneously cushion the ball into the body by pulling both hands into the waist. This will give 'soft hands' which will lead to cleaner and smoother fielding.

Centring the Ball
(Fig 48)

Infielders should always try to concentrate on keeping the ball in the centre of the body, and keeping their backsides low to the ground. Once the ball has been cleanly fielded, the infielder is ready to throw.

Skip and Throw
(Figs 49 & 50)

The skip and throw technique will allow infielders to throw the ball as quickly and accurately as possible.

While the infielder cushions the ball into the body, he should begin to position himself to throw it. The glove-side shoulder and hip should be lined up with the target. This will result in a side-on position ready to throw the ball.

Next the throwing-side foot should pivot sideways, so that the inside of the foot is facing the target (right foot for right-handers, left foot for left-handers).

The player should then take a short hop towards the target on the throwing-side foot, then as the other leg lands, he should make a strong accurate throw pivoting over the top of it.

Fig 48   The infielder centring the ball.

Fig 49 Pivoting into a side-on position to make the throw.

Fig 50 The throwing position.

Follow Through
(Fig 51)

After the throw the player should follow through, pointing the throwing-side shoulder towards the target, and lifting the back leg off the ground. The momentum should carry the thrower towards the target.

FIRST BASE

The first baseman's primary responsibility is to be a fielder. If the ball is hit towards the first base area, he will have to field it and make the correct play. If the ball is hit on the infield away from the first baseman, he has another specific role to perform.

45

Fig 51   The follow through.

The first baseman should assume a position whereby he can get to the base in plenty of time to catch any ball thrown towards it.

Playing the Base
(Fig 52)

When the ball is hit on the infield away from the first baseman, he has to get to first base as quickly as possible. The non-glove foot should be placed on or next to it. He then turns towards the player who fielded the ball, and provides a big target for the thrower to aim for. To do this he should hold his glove out in front.

The first baseman should attempt to catch all balls with two hands. However,

Fig 52   The first baseman's position.

Square Drill
Objectives To develop quick hands and accurate throwing technique.
Equipment Gloves and baseballs.
Drill Four players stand in a square 30ft (9m) apart. Simply start throwing the ball around the square in a clock-wise direction. The more advanced the players, the greater the speed of the drill. This can also be done in an anti-clockwise direction.
Coaching points Catch the ball with two hands.
Quick transfer of ball to throwing hand.
Insist on correct mechanics.
Insist on quickness and quality of throws.

Fig 53   Holding the runner on first base.

often throws are inaccurate, and it is the first baseman's job to field all balls regardless of how well they are thrown. This may require him to use only one hand for expedience.

Holding the Base Runner
(Fig 53)

If there is a runner on first base, the first baseman has to attempt to hold the runner as close to the base as possible, to make it harder for him to steal second base. If held close to first base, then there is further to go to get to second. This will subsequently give the catcher more time to throw out the base stealer.

Pepper
Objectives Practice throwing, fielding and bat control.
Equipment Bat, gloves and baseballs.
Drill One batter, five fielders. Fielder throws the ball to the hitter, who using a half swing hits the ball back to the fielders. They field the ball, throw it back to the batter and the drill continues.
Coaching points Hitters focus on bat control.
Fielders concentrate on good fielding and throwing mechanics.
Drill should be performed quickly and precisely.

In most instances the first baseman will actually position himself on the base, making the runner stay close to avoid being picked off by the pitcher.

SECOND BASE AND SHORTSTOP

Collectively known as the pivot or middle infielders, these players are generally very athletic, making quick plays with accurate throws. These players field either side of second base. Their primary responsibility is to field any ground balls hit through the middle of the diamond, and make accurate throws to the appropriate base.

The term 'pivot' comes from the way these two players execute double plays. This occurs when two runners are put out in one play.

If the ball is hit between first and second base, it is usually the responsibility of the second baseman to field the ball. If there is a runner on first base, the second baseman will attempt to initiate a double play by throwing the ball to the shortstop, who will have moved towards second base. The shortstop will then touch second base, and quickly throw the ball to first base. If successful two players will be out, the runner who was on first, and the batter.

Conversely, if the ball is hit between second base and third base, the shortstop will field the ball and throw to the second baseman, who will have moved towards second base. The second baseman will then relay the ball on to the first baseman.

The middle infielders are generally the best fielders on the team, being very quick and agile, with 'soft hands' and strong, accurate throwing arms.

Situation Defence
Objectives To simulate game situations.
Equipment Full playing equipment.
Drill With a full infield the coach calls out the number of outs, inning and position of base runners. He then hits the ball and the infield make the appropriate play. In this drill you can use real or imaginary base runners.
Coaching points Infielders should know what to do before the ball is put into play. The catcher should call the plays.

THIRD BASE

The third baseman generally does not have to field the ball as often as middle infielders. However, he must be able to field balls that are hit very hard, and make strong accurate throws.

Third base is known as the 'hot corner', because the majority of batters are right-handed: when they hit the ball hard, it is generally pulled down the third baseline, towards the third baseman. Therefore the third baseman has to have very quick reflexes and a lot of courage to get behind these hard-hit balls.

The throw from third base to first base is the longest across the diamond, therefore the third baseman has to have a strong arm to be able to make these throws.

The third baseman will also initiate double plays, when the ball is hit towards him with a runner on first. Like the shortstop, the third baseman will field the ball, and throw to the second baseman, who will step on second base, then relay the ball to the first baseman.

6
Outfield

The outfield is made up of three fielders, the left fielder, the centre fielder and the right fielder. These three players make up the last line of defence, covering the largest area of the field.

POSITIONING
(Fig 54)

Generally the left fielder will be positioned between the third baseman and the short-stop, the centre fielder will be slightly to the right or to the left of second base and

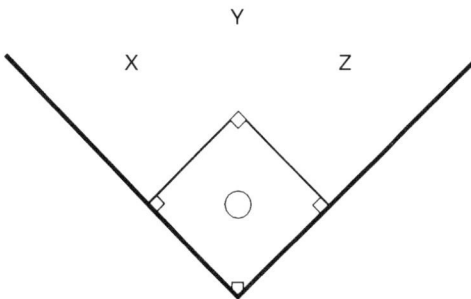

X Left fielder

Y Centre fielder

Z Right fielder

Coach Hit Drill
Objectives Outfielders field different types of balls and practise hitting the cut-off.
Equipment Balls, glove and a bat.
Drill The coach hits balls to the out-fielders. He can hit fly balls, grounders, line drives etc. The outfielders must field the ball and throw to a cut-off sit-uated between the coach and the out-fielders. The cut-off relays the ball to a catcher who feeds the coach.
Coaching points Get into position early.
Catch the ball while moving forwards.
Hit the cut-off.
Catch every ball possible.

---

the right fielder will be between the second baseman and the first baseman.

These are the general positions, but they will alter slightly to accommodate several factors.

Strengths of the Batter

If the batter consistently hits the ball to a specific part of the field, it is logical to position the fielders to defend that particular area. For example, if a batter

Fig 54   The standard outfield position.

consistently pulls the ball down the left field line, the left fielder will move closer to the line to get ready for any balls hit in that direction. Consequently the centre fielder and right fielder will move over as well, so that the centre fielder may be positioned behind the shortstop, and the right fielder behind the second baseman. This will leave an area in right field unguarded. However, we have already decided that the batter is very unlikely to hit towards the right field, so we are prepared to take that risk.

The Game Situation

For example, the game is in the bottom of the ninth inning, scores tied, and the winning run is on third base with no outs. If the outfield play at normal positions, the runner will score on a base hit or a sacrifice fly (the ball will be caught, but the run will be scored). Therefore the outfield will play closer to the infield, giving them a chance to throw the runner out at home plate. They are prepared to let the batter take the chance to hit it over their heads, which will score the winning run. At normal depth the outfield would probably catch the ball, but the runner would have 'tagged up' and scored by that time, winning the game anyway.

Right- or Left-handed Batter

Depending which way round the batter hits, the outfield will shift slightly to accommodate this. Right-handers have the tendency to hit towards left field, with left-handers generally hitting towards right field. The defence will usually play towards these areas, hoping that the batter will hit true to form, with them in the position to play defence.

FLY BALLS
(Fig 55)

The main job of the outfielder is to catch fly balls – any balls that are hit in the air. When a fly ball is caught the batter is automatically out.

The glove should be held above the shoulders with the fingers pointing up. Players should be encouraged to catch the ball with both hands, placing the throwing hand by the thumb of the glove; this will make the players catch the ball directly over their heads.

Fig 55   The position for catching fly balls.

50

while moving forwards. This will enable him to throw the ball more quickly and also provide momentum, which will give a stronger throw.

Basket Catch
(Fig 56)

No matter how fast a player can run, there will always be instances where the ball will fall in front of him. In this situation the best way to catch the ball is to use a basket catch. The glove is held out at about waist height, with the fingers of the glove pointing downwards. Again the player should attempt to catch the ball with both hands, securing it with the throwing hand.

When the ball is caught the player should squeeze the glove to ensure the ball does not pop out. The throwing hand can then remove the ball from the glove ready to throw.

Judging Fly Balls

It can sometimes be very difficult to judge a fly ball: wind, sun and background interference can make the job of the outfielder very difficult. Despite these problems, the outfielder will be expected to make the catches.

As a general rule the outfielder should try to keep the ball in front of him at all times. When the ball contacts the bat, the outfielder should take three steps back. If the ball is hit in front of him, it is relatively easy for the outfielder to run forwards to catch the ball; it is far more difficult to catch the ball running backwards.

Even if the outfielder is in the exact position to catch the ball, he should still take three steps back, then take the catch

Fig 56   The basket catch.

51

This is a difficult skill to master, and where possible players should always catch the ball over their heads.

OUTFIELD GROUNDERS
(Fig 57)

The outfield is a large area and not all balls will be hit in the air. Often balls will come to the outfielders along the ground. As the last line of defence, it is vital that outfielders can competently field this type of ball.

If there are runners on base the out-fielder has to field and throw the ball as quickly as possible to the infield. The method of fielding a ground ball in this situation is the same as that for an infielder. Ideally the outfielder should field the ball while moving forwards, which will speed up the play and enable him to generate forward momentum for a stronger throw.

If there are no runners on base the out-fielder will have more time to field the ball. In this situation the blocking method can be used, which makes fielding the ball easier (*see* Fig 57).

Fig 57   The long barrier position.

THROWING TO THE INFIELD

Once the outfielder has fielded the ball, the next task is to throw the ball to the infield. With runners on base it is vital for the outfielder to make a strong, accurate throw ahead of the runners to stop them advancing. In most situations the outfielders will be aiming for a 'cut-off man', who will relay the ball to the required base. Cut-offs and relays will be discussed in Chapter 9.

COMMUNICATION

It is vital to have communication and teamwork between outfielders. When catching a ball the player should shout 'I got it' and wave his arms in a circular motion. This is essentially to let the rest of the team know that he is catching the ball, and that they should get out of the way.

When an outfielder has called for a ball, the other outfielders should be ready to back him up, in case he misjudges or misplays the ball.

Drop and Go
Objectives To teach the drop step and sprint to the ball.
Equipment Balls and gloves.
Drill The player stands 30ft (9m) from the coach. The coach throws the ball over the player's shoulder. The player does a drop step, sprints to the ball, and catches it.
Coaching points Look once and go. Throw over both shoulders.

7
Batting and Bunting

It has been said that the single most difficult skill in sport is to hit a baseball. The combination of a round bat, round ball and pitchers using different speeds, locations and trajectories on the ball, make hitting a baseball very difficult. Even the best hitters in the Major Leagues will only hit the ball safely three out of every ten attempts.

To be a successful hitter, the batter must possess several athletic qualities: hand-eye co-ordination, quick reflexes, speed, power, kinaesthetic awareness and confidence. Even then, hitting is an activity doomed to failure, in that even a good batter will only succeed 30 per cent of the time. Batters need to be aware of this statistic so the feeling of making a good hit makes the effort worthwhile.

BAT SELECTION

For batting efficiently the correct selection of bat is of paramount importance. It is vital that beginners realize that it is bat speed and timing that determine how hard the ball is hit. Often beginners will select the heaviest bat available; however if the bat is too heavy it will be detrimental to the swing, and will reduce batting efficiency.

Batters should select a bat that they feel comfortable with. It should be light enough to swing quickly, but stable enough to enable a good contact.

GRIP
(Figs 58 & 59)

It is very important that the bat is gripped correctly. An incorrect grip will impair the batter's ability to swing through the ball, thereby reducing the overall efficiency of the swing.

Fig 58   The bat handle should rest on the middle of the fingers.

hitter may be able to compensate for an incorrectly weighted bat by 'choking up' the bat. This entails the batter gripping the bat further up the handle away from the knob. This will then give the bat balance, and the batter more control.

STANCE

Distance from the Plate
(Fig 61)

The distance the batter stands from the plate depends mostly on body size. The batter should stand far enough away from the plate so that the top of the bat passes slightly over the outside corner of the plate when the hitter's arms are

Fig 59   The batting grip.

The bat should be gripped like an axe, with the hands together. The handle of the bat should rest along the middle of the fingers, not in the palms of the hands.

When holding the bat, the batter should grip firmly enough to maintain control of the bat, but loosely enough to keep the hands relaxed. It is common to see inexperienced batters squeezing the bat as hard as they can. This is counter-productive as it will only lead to a tense, tight swing.

Choking Up
(Fig 60)

Many teams will not have a great number of bats to choose from. However, the

Fig 60   Choking up.

Fig 61   The batting position in relation to the plate.

extended. Standing too close to the plate may cause the hitter to cramp up and not get full extension of the arms. Standing too far from the plate will prevent the hitter from reaching pitches that are on the outer part of the plate.

Body Position
(Figs 62 & 63)

The batter's groin should be in line with the centre of the plate. The stance should be slightly closed with the hitter's front foot slightly closer to the plate than the back foot. This will put the batter into position to hit all kinds of pitch. The batter's hips should be parallel to the plate, and the front shoulder should stay down.

The position of the hitter's hands and arms are important during batting. The hands should be relaxed, to prevent the batter from tensing up. Note the angle of the bat in Fig 63, and that the front shoulder is down.

A common fault with beginners is to have the bat resting on the shoulder. All this succeeds in doing is adding to the batter's problems. From this point the bat has to be moved before the swing can commence. Subsequently the time the

Fig 62   The batter's body position.

Fig 63   The position of the batter's head and arms.

batter has to make a decision and to swing is reduced, giving the pitcher an added advantage.

BATTING TECHNIQUE

Stride and Swing
(Figs 64–67)

The stride provides the momentum for the swing. Often coaches will tell players to stride and swing; in fact, the batter should stride *to* swing.

Tee Drill
Objectives To work on the batter's swing.
Equipment Balls, bat and batting tee (or traffic cone). Fence or net to hit the ball into.
Drill A ball is placed on the tee, the player takes his swing, and hits the ball. Obviously the ball is stationary, so the player can concentrate on mechanics.
Coaching points Work on correct mechanics and swing.

57

Fig 64   The feet position in the batting stance.

Fig 65   The stride position.

Fig 66   The position of the hands
during the swing.

Fig 67   The head should be kept still
during the swing.

The stride does not have to be very big. Often a big stride will result in the batter lunging at the ball. Usually, the stride need only be small, as it is simply to generate the momentum for the swing.

At this stage it is important to keep the hands back in a power position from where they can explode forwards. As the hands move forwards to contact the ball, the hips should turn quickly with the back toe pivoting.

During the swing the front shoulder should remain low, and the head must stay still. It is also important that the hips and shoulders do not turn upwards. This should keep the swing flat, preventing the batter from popping up. The head should stay down, eyes watching the ball on to the bat.

Follow Through
(Fig 68)

As the bat contacts the ball the elbows and wrists should fully extend, in order to impart the maximum force possible on the ball. The hitter should feel like he is throwing the bat at the ball.

After contact the batter should 'pull' the bat through the ball to follow

59

Fig 68   The follow through.

through. The follow through should not be restricted in any way as this will limit the swing and subsequently the batter's success.

The batter should be balanced all the way through the hitting sequence. Once the ball has been hit the batter should drop the bat, and drive out of the box towards first base. Note that the bat should be dropped not thrown, as this can be very dangerous.

STRIKE ZONE
(Fig 69)

All hitters should endeavour to learn their own strike zone. It is very important that hitters are disciplined and do not swing for pitches that are out of the strike zone. Even if the batter does connect in this situation, it is probable that it will not be a solid connection, and the ball will be hit weakly. Hitters should be patient and wait for a pitch they want to hit. It is vital that they do not give away strikes to the pitcher.

Hitters should also hit the ball where it is pitched. If the ball is pitched on the outside part of the plate the batter should drive the ball to that side of the field. He should not try to pull the ball over. Similarly, if the ball is pitched inside, the hitter should pull the ball. By hitting a ball where it is pitched the hitter's chance of success is increased.

PHILOSOPHY

Hitters should always go to the plate wanting to hit. Often hitters will go to bat hoping to get a walk, which is unlikely to happen. Hitters should rather be aggressive at the plate, concentrating on their strike zone. When the ball comes into the zone they should hit it hard. This aggression must be controlled, however, as it is

Fig 69   The strike zone.

Soft Toss
Objectives To work on mechanics and swing.
Equipment Balls, bat, fence or net.
Drill Coach sits at the side of the batter and tosses balls towards the batter. The batter takes his normal swing, hitting the ball into the net.
Coaching points Work on correct mechanics of the swing.
Hit through the ball.
Aim for line drives.

no use swinging wildly at pitches; this is likely to result in strike outs.

Overall, batting is a very difficult skill to master. Players should work on their swing in practice, so that when they go to the plate during a game they are concentrating on the pitcher and the baseball, and not distracting themselves thinking about different aspects of the swing.

BUNTING

A bunt is a special type of batting technique where the ball is hit misleadingly

61

Bunt Pepper
Objectives To practise bunting.
Equipment Bats and balls.
Drill As regular pepper (p.47). Instead of the half swing, the batter should square and bunt the ball.
Coaching points Correct bunt mechanics.
Feed must be good.

Fig 70 The sacrifice bunt: the feet pivot and the right hand slides up the bat.

softly. The purpose of a bunt is either to reach base safely or to advance a runner into scoring position. There are two types of bunt: the sacrifice bunt where the bunter will sacrifice himself in order to advance a runner and the drag bunt where the bunter will attempt to reach first base safely. The former is generally used when there are runners on first and second base who have to be advanced: a properly executed sacrifice bunt will make it very difficult for the defence to throw out the lead runner, even if the batter is caught out. The drag bunt can be a useful tactic early on in a game, for example, when there is not much pressure and no runners on base.

Sacrifice Bunt

MECHANICS
(Figs 70 & 71)
The sequence for a sacrifice bunt is as follows:
1. As the pitcher starts his delivery, the hitter pivots his feet.
2. The hitter slides his upper hand along the barrel of the bat approximately 12in (30cm). It is vital that the upper hand holds the bat as shown in Fig 70 to protect the fingers and also to help deaden the ball.
3. The hitter gets the bat out in front at waist level.

4. The knees bend and the hitter is in a semi-crouched position.
5. The hitter allows the ball to hit the bat. It is important that he does not push the bat onto the ball.

If done correctly this will cause the ball to come off the bat softly, thus enabling the base runners to advance.

In sacrifice bunting it is important that the hitter only bunts strikes. By attempting to bunt balls, the batter may bunt poorly, giving the advantage to the fielding team.

Ideally the batter should bunt the ball successfully on the first attempt. This will

Fig 71   The sacrifice bunt: the batter covers the strike zone with the bat.

Bunting Accuracy
Objectives To practice bunting down the base lines.
Equipment Bats and balls.
Drill Four players: one bunter, one pitcher, two fielders. Fielders are placed 3ft (90cm) inside the foul lines. The pitcher pitches the ball, the bunter must bunt between the fielder and the foul line. If successful he scores five points. If the bunt is inside the fielders, minus five. If the bunt is foul minus one. If the bunt is popped up, minus ten points. After ten bunts the players swap positions. The player with the highest total is the winner.
Coaching points Bunt the ball down the lines.
Bunt the ball on the ground.

Two-Man Bunt Drill
Objectives To teach the fundamentals of bunting.
Equipment Bats and balls.
Drill Two players, 20ft (6m) apart; player A is the batter, B the thrower. B throws the ball, A squares round and bunts. After ten bunts the players swap places.
Coaching points Catch the ball on the bat.
Get the bat out in front.

make the defence play 'honest', that is not specifically trying to defend the bunt, as they will not be prepared for it. The bunt should be down the base lines just in fair territory. If the ball is bunted back towards the pitcher, it makes it relatively easy for the pitcher to throw out the lead runner.

Finally neither the batter nor the runner should attempt to run until after the ball hits the ground. This will help ensure that the batter concentrates on a good bunt, and prevent the runner being doubled up.

Drag Bunt

The drag bunt is meant to produce base hits. It is therefore necessary to disguise the drag bunt until the last possible moment, so that the defence has no clues as to what to expect.

63

Fig 72   The drag bunt: the right-handed batter steps back with his right foot and slides his right hand up the bat.

Fig 73   The batter must leave for first base as soon as he hits the ball.

DRAG BUNT SEQUENCE
(Figs 72 & 73)
1. Step back with right foot, bending both knees.
2. Slide right hand up the bat, extending the bat over the plate.
3. Bunt the ball down the third base line.
4. Run towards first base.

Good consistent bunting can increase a team's overall run production. It gives the team another option, giving the defence more to think about.

8

Base Running

As soon as the batter puts the ball into play, he becomes a base runner. If a team has good base runners, it will tend to put the defence under pressure. A lot of runs can be scored through good base running.

FIRST BASE
(Figs 74–76)

Once the batter has put the ball into play, he should drive out of the batter's box towards first base. Even weak hits to the infield can be turned into base hits if the runner has speed and runs the ball out, beating the throw.

When running to first base on a ball hit to the infield, the runner can run straight through first base. It is important that runners should run through the base rather than round it , as this will get them quicker to the next base. After running through the base, the runner must turn right into foul territory. If the runner beats the throw, then turns to the left towards infield to get to second base, he may be tagged out by the fielding team.

Rounding First Base

When any ball is hit to the outfield, the runner should be thinking of trying for second base. About 15–20ft (4.5–6m) from first base, the runner should start a sweep, first outwards, then towards the

base. The runner's momentum will then be towards second base. The runner should run through first base and advance approximately one third of the way to second. He should be looking for a misfield or a bobble by the outfielder, then make up his mind whether to go to second or return to first base.

Fig 74   Leading into first base.

Fig 75   Looking for any overthrows.

Fig 76   Turning to the right at first base is essential to avoid being tagged out.

FIRST BASE SITUATIONS

Leads
(Fig 77)

Leads are the steps the base runner takes from one base towards the next one, and come in two parts: the primary lead and the secondary lead. The primary lead is taken before the pitcher pitches, and the secondary lead after.

PRIMARY LEAD
The standard primary lead from first base should be three and a half strides, or whatever the runner feels comfortable

Overrun First Base
Objectives To teach players to overrun first base every time.
Equipment Home plate and first base.
Drill Players should be in their normal batting stance in the batter's box. The batter takes an imaginary swing, then sprints to and through first base. When the player touches first base, he should turn his head right, to look for any overthrows. The player should then join the back of the line.
Coaching points Run straight through first base.
Turn to the right every time.

with, taken when the pitcher is in the set position. Whatever the lead, the runner must be able to get back to first base to avoid being picked off by the pitcher.

The runner's feet should be about shoulder width apart, with the weight on the balls of the feet. This will enable the runner to move quickly in any direction. He should lean slightly back towards first base in readiness for any pick-off move.

While taking this primary lead it is vital that the runner watches the pitcher at all times. If the runner moves off the base without watching the pitcher, he is likely to fall victim to a pick-off move.

SECONDARY LEAD

Once the pitcher has started his motion towards home plate the runner can then take a secondary lead – three or four steps towards second base. If the ball is hit this will give the runner a good jump towards second. However, the runner must ensure that the pitcher is actually going to throw to the plate, (he may wait till the ball has left the pitcher's hand) and that he can get back to first before the catcher can throw him out.

Stealing Second Base

Before stealing (advancing a base without the ball being hit) the runner must ensure that the pitcher is going to the plate. If he attempts to steal too early, the pitcher will be able to pick him off. If he delays too long, the catcher will be able to throw him out at second.

Fig 77   The primary lead.

As soon as the pitcher motions towards home, the runner should go. If the pitcher then 'cheats' and throws the ball to first it is a balk, and the runner will automatically be given second base.

From the primary lead position, the runner is then ready to steal. First the head and upper body will turn towards second base, and the legs should drive towards second. The runner should stay low and go directly for second base. He should not attempt to locate the ball as this will only slow him down.

When the runner is about 15ft (4.5m) from the base he should begin his slide into the base either feet first or head first.

Fly Balls

When a batter hits a fly ball to the outfield with less than two outs, the runner on first base should move approximately half-way down the base line towards second base. If the ball is caught, he will be able to return comfortably to first base. If the ball is not caught then he should easily make second base, possibly third.

SECOND BASE SITUATIONS

Leads

The primary lead at second base depends on the position of the second baseman and the shortstop. The further they are away from the base, the greater the lead should be. However the runner must be ready for any pick-off moves by the pitcher.

As the pitcher pitches, the runner should take a secondary lead towards third base. This will give him a good jump, and should enable him to score on a base hit. It should also be relatively comfortable to return to second base if necessary.

Fly Balls

With only one out, if the ball is hit to deep right field or centre field, the runner should tag up, that is he should return to second base from his lead position to avoid being thrown out, and try to advance to third on the throw. If the ball is hit to left field, the runner should move about a third of the way towards third base. If the outfielder misplays the ball the runner can advance, and possibly score. If the ball is caught, the runner has sufficient time to return to second base.

THIRD BASE SITUATIONS

Leads

The lead at third base should be in foul territory. If the runner takes a lead in fair territory and is hit by a batted ball he is out. If a batted ball hits the runner in foul territory the ball is dead.

Lead off and go
Objectives To teach correct lead–off.
Equipment Bases.
Drills Players take a lead from first base. The coach, acting as a pitcher, makes a move to the plate. On the first move the player takes a secondary lead, then goes on an imaginary hit and run.
Coaching points Do not leave too early.
Runner should go to third base.

If the pitcher pitches from the set position, the runner should take a primary lead similar to that at first base. As the pitcher delivers the ball the runner can then take a secondary lead. If the pitcher uses a full wind-up, the runner should take a walking lead. However he must ensure that he is close enough to third base to avoid being picked off by a throw from the catcher.

Ground Balls

If the ball is hit on the ground the runner will have to decide whether to try to score or stay at third. This decision will be influenced by three factors:

1. Position of the infielders.
2. Speed of the ball.
3. Game situation.

If the infielders are playing in, it is unlikely that the runner will be able to score, unless an error is made or the ball bounces erratically. If the ball is hit hard, this again gives the fielders an advantage, because it will give the runner less time to get to home plate. The game situation will also affect the runner's decision. If strong hitters are coming up to bat, the runner will be less inclined to attempt to score and risk being thrown out. However if weaker hitters are due up, the runner may be more inclined to take the risk.

Fly Balls
(Fig 78)

Runners on third base should tag up on all fly balls. Once the ball is caught the runner can leave the base and try to score. If the ball is hit moderately deeply, the runner will score with relative ease. If

the ball is hit for a base hit, the runner will also score easily.

It is definitely not worth the risk of not tagging up, as the player will have nothing to lose by doing so.

SLIDING

All good base runners can slide well. It is an important skill that ideally needs to be mastered by all players.

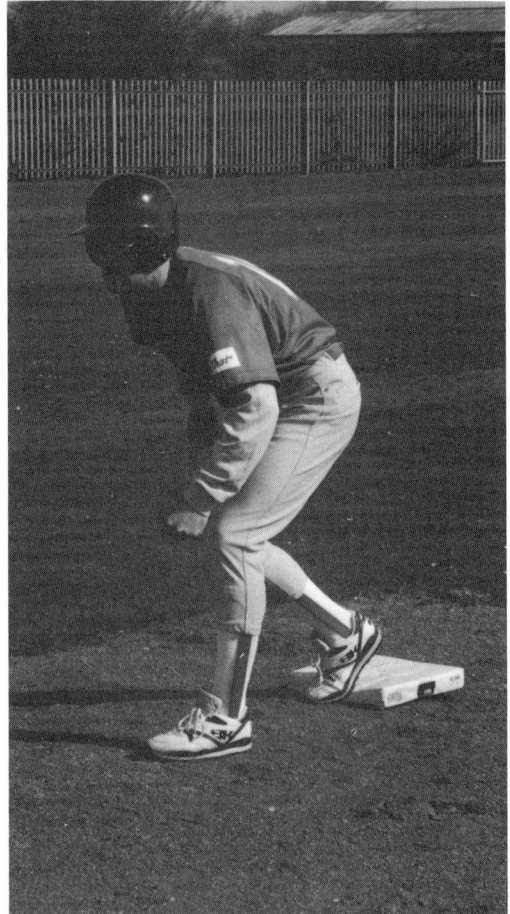

Fig 78   Tagging up at third base, ready to go home.

There are three main reasons why base runners need to slide, they are:

1. To stop at the base. First base is the only base that the runner can overrun. If he overruns second or third, he can be tagged out.
2. To avoid being tagged out. Sliding into base makes the fielder's task of making a tag more difficult.
3. To break up a double play. In a double play situation it is the base runner's responsibility to attempt to prevent the pivot player from making a good throw.

Bent Leg Slide
(Fig 79)

For the bent leg slide, the runner slides into base feet first. Most runners tend to favour this type of slide as it is generally safe.

When sliding the runners must remember that it is not a jump at the base. A slide should be controlled and well timed. In most situations the slide should start 9–12ft (3–4m) from the base. The runner should not start his slide too early, as he will not make the base. Conversely he should not make the slide too late, as this may make it easier for the fielder to make the tag. It may also cause the runner to overrun the base.

At the start of the slide, the runner should bend the take-off leg under his body, while extending the lead leg. He should then slide on the outside of the bent leg. As he hits the floor, he should throw his head and arms backwards. This ensures that he stays low.

The runner should always touch the base with the lead leg, keeping it slightly flexed, and the heel off the ground. This allows him to regain his feet quickly, so he can advance if there is a bad throw.

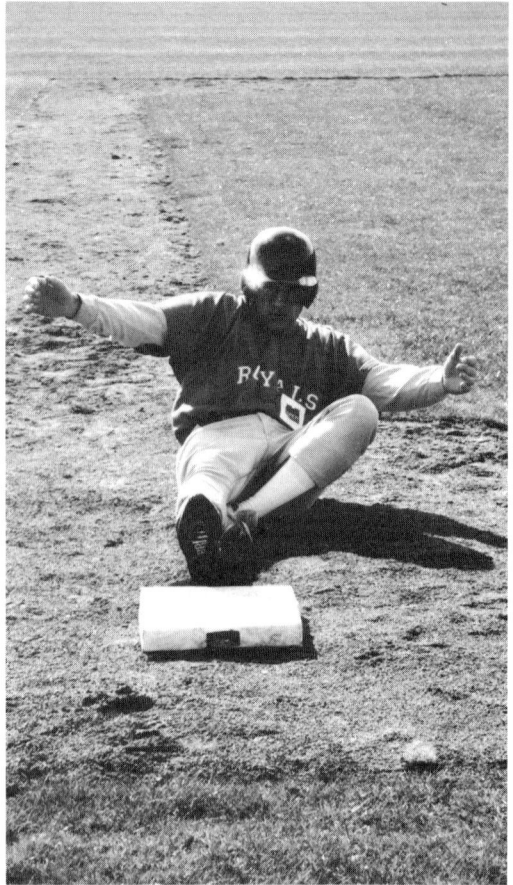

Fig 79   The bent leg slide.

Head First Slide
(Fig 80)

The head first slide is generally only used by more advanced players; it is safer to teach children and beginners the feet first slide.

In the head first slide the runner again starts to slide about 9–12ft (3–4m) from the base. This type of slide is faster than the feet first slide. As the runner hits the floor both arms are extended. The feet should be kept off the ground, so that the slide is mainly on the chest and stomach. In most base-stealing situations, where the runner has very little time, this type of slide will be used.

Hook Slide
(Fig 81)

The hook slide is generally used to avoid a tag. The slide can be to either side of the base, the choice being determined by the position of the fielder. Therefore it is important that players can slide on either side.

When the slide starts the runner should attempt to get into a prone position as quickly as possible. The lead leg should be extended, the body should be turned slightly away from the base. The instep of the back foot should be used to tag the base. The lead leg should be extended, but kept away from the fielder, giving the fielder only one leg to tag.

Fade Away Slide

The fade away slide is essentially the same as the hook slide, but is performed further away from the base. As the runner slides past the base, he should tag it with his left hand.

This is an effective method of avoiding a tag as it gives the fielder practically nothing to tag.

Fig 80   The head first slide.

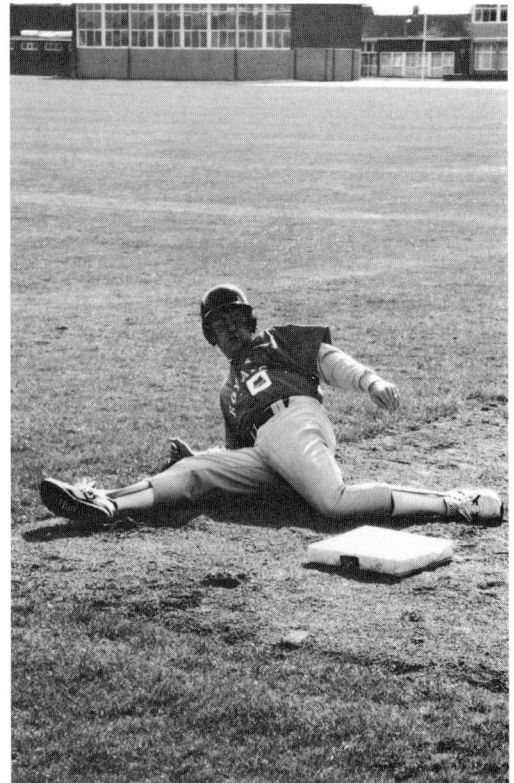

Fig 81   The hook slide.

Breaking up the Double Play

A base runner can try to break up a double play by throwing the pivot fielder off balance. To do this legally, he must ensure that he is within touching distance of the base when contact is made with the fielder.

The hook slide is usually used to break up the double play, in that the runner attempts to contact the planted leg of the pivot man. Ideally this will force the pivot man to avoid the slide, which may cause a bad throw, a weak throw or no throw at all. Either way the runner must try to protect his team mate.

9
Team Play

TEAM DEFENCE

The objective of all defensive strategy is primarily to prevent runs being scored, and the advancement of runners into scoring positions. Fielders should understand these objectives and follow these general guidelines:

1. Always keep the ball in front of them.
2. If they cannot catch the ball, knock it down.
3. Throw ahead of the runner.
4. Make accurate throws.

Within this framework there are specific defences to combat specific positions.

Pop Fly Coverage
(Fig 82)

This area of defence requires the whole team to understand the general rules.

1. Players must always call for a fly ball 'I got it' loud and clear.
2. Centre fielder has priority over all other fielders.
3. All outfielders have priority over the infielders.
4. Infielders have priority over the catcher.
5. First and third basemen should make all catches near the mound, in front of home plate, down the side lines and near the dug-outs.

6. Shortstop and second basemen should catch all balls down the left field and right field lines respectively, behind the bases.
7. Catchers should catch pop-ups behind the plate that other infielders cannot handle.
8. Unless it is absolutely necessary, the pitcher should not catch pop flies.

Relays and Cut-Offs

These defensive plays require a lot of practice. By executing them correctly, the defence may stop runners taking an extra base, keep them out of scoring position and set up double play possibilities. Relays and cut-offs are used when the ball is hit to the outfield with runners on base.

CUT-OFFS
The role of the cut-off is to act as a target man for the outfielder. Purely by being in the correct position the cut-off may prevent runners from trying to take an extra base.

For all plays the cut-off should stand with his hands above his head giving the outfielder a good target. The cut-off has to receive the ball and quickly relay it to the correct base; he will be told by the respective baseman where to throw the ball or even if he should hold the ball and not make a throw. The instructions to the cut-off should be loud and clear.

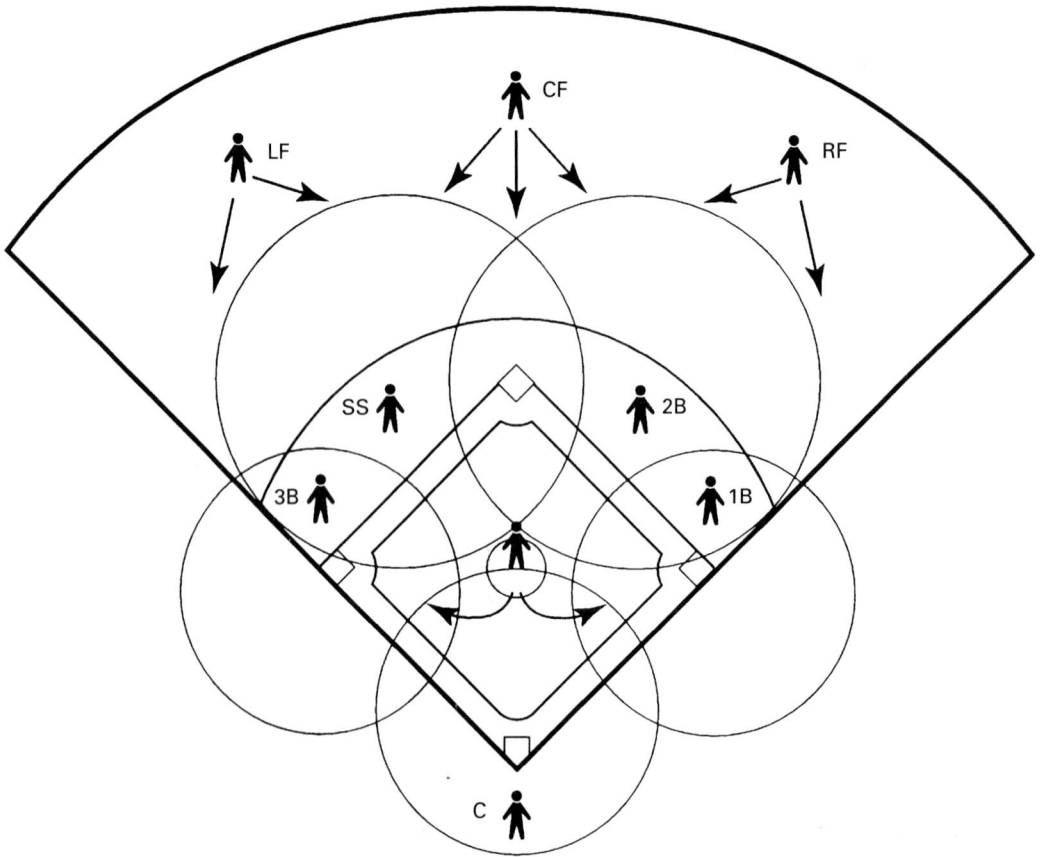

Fig 82   Pop fly coverage (see Fig 1, page 14 for key to abbreviations).

For example, if there is a runner on first base and the batter hits a single to centre field, the shortstop will be the cut-off. The aim is to prevent the runner from advancing to third base. The shortstop should assume a position about 40ft (12m) in front of third base. The centre fielder should throw to third base aiming for the cut-off man's head. If the throw is on tar-get and can get the lead runner, the third baseman should not say anything, and the shortstop should not intercept the ball but let it go directly to third base.

If the throw is on line but not strong enough, the third baseman will shout 'Relay, relay'. The shortstop should cut the ball and relay it to third base. If the runner is definitely going to make third base, the third baseman should shout 'Cut'. If the cut-off hears nothing else he should keep the ball and run back towards the infield. However, if the batter tries to get to second base, the shout will be 'Cut 2' and the cut-off will relay the ball to second base.

The cut-off is important, because if the outfielder throws a long arcing throw to third base, missing the cut-off, the runner will probably be safe at third, and the batter will get into scoring position at second base.

The cut-offs for the various plays are as follows:

Plays to home
Hit to right field: first baseman
Hit to centre field: first baseman
Hit to left field: third baseman

Plays to third
Hit to right field: shortstop
Hit to centre field: shortstop

Bunt Defence

There are set defences for specific situations.

RUNNER ON FIRST
(Fig 83)
The aim is to put out the lead runner; if that is not possible it is best to get the runner going to first. In this situation the catcher, pitcher, first baseman and third baseman will charge in to try to field the ball. The second baseman covers first base, the shortstop covers second, the catcher covers third. The outfielders back up first and second base.

RUNNERS ON FIRST AND SECOND
(Fig 84)
The aim is to put out the lead runner at third base. If this is not possible, the

Fig 83 Bunt coverage – runner on first base (see page 14 for key).

defence should try to get any of the other runners.

The catcher will try to reach any balls. The pitcher will cover the third base line, the first baseman will charge and cover the first base line. The second baseman will cover first base, the shortstop will cover second, and the third baseman will cover third. The left fielder backs up third, the centre fielder backs up second, and the right fielder backs up first.

Fig 84 Bunt coverage – runners on first and second bases (see page 14 for key).

75

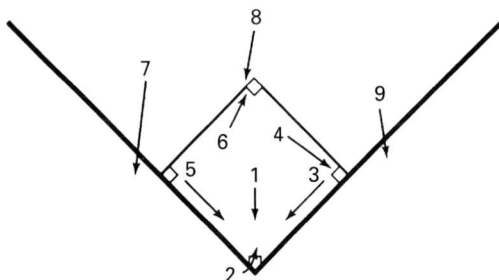

Fig 85   Bunt coverage – runner on third base (suicide squeeze). (See page 14 for key.)

RUNNER ON THIRD (SUICIDE SQUEEZE)
(Fig 85)

The aim is to get the runner out at the plate. If this is not possible the defence will try to get the runner going to first.

The catcher covers the plate. The pitcher, first baseman and third baseman charge to catch the ball, the second baseman covers first, the shortstop covers second. The right fielder will back up first base, the centre fielder backs up second and the left fielder backs up third.

If the runner breaks too early, the pitcher can throw the ball high and outside, so that the batter cannot put the ball into play. This will let the catcher field the ball and tag the incoming runner.

TEAM OFFENCE

Team offence is vital to successful baseball teams. This entails the batting team using various plays to advance runners and to score runs. Teams who can use bunts, hit and runs, steals and squeeze plays effectively will often be successful.

Aggressive offence can intimidate the opposition into making mistakes, which will eventually lead to runs being scored.

Bunt

The purpose of a sacrifice bunt is to advance players into scoring position. For example, if there is a runner on first base and a weak hitter at the plate, a successful bunt will advance the runner to second base. From second the runner should score on any subsequent base hit. As the batter is likely to be out, this strategy will normally only be used with no outs.

A second bunt situation can occur with runners on first and second with no outs. Towards the end of a close game the batter may want to advance the runners to second and third base respectively. This will allow the runner on third to score on a sacrifice fly or a squeeze, or both runners to score on a base hit.

When bunting it is vital to avoid the double play. The bunt must be good: on the ground near the base lines. Runners must not break for the next base until the ball hits the ground.

Suicide Squeeze

The suicide squeeze occurs with a runner on third base, usually with less than two outs, and late in a close game.

When the pitcher begins his delivery the runner should be ready to break for home. However, the runner should wait until the pitcher is just about to release the ball, which will hopefully prevent him from changing the pitch. As the runner is committed to going for home, the batter must contact the ball, even if he can only foul it off. If the batter fails to connect, the runner will be stranded between the bases. If the ball is bunted onto the ground in fair territory, the runner will cross the plate before the defence can make a play. However, if the ball is bunted up into the air the defence can make an easy double play.

Stealing Second Base

Stealing second base can occur at any time in the game. Ideally a fast runner should be at first. The best pitch to steal on would be a breaking ball, such as a curveball. This type of pitch would give the runner more time to get to second. By stealing second base, the runner puts himself into a scoring position, so that he will score on any base hits.

Hit and Run

The hit and run is a very effective play for advancing runners. With a runner on first base and the pitcher behind in the count – in these situations a fastball is likely, as this is an easy pitch to control – the hit and run is a good offensive play.

As the pitcher motions towards the plate, the runner will take off towards second. The batter's job is to protect the runner by hitting the ball on the ground. As the runner breaks towards second, hopefully the second baseman will also break to cover the steal. This will leave a gap through which the batter can hit the ball. If the batter hits the gap, the runner should make third base and the hitter should be on first.

It is vital that the batter avoids the double play. The ball should be hit on the ground behind the runner.

10
Role of the Manager and Coach

As the manager of a baseball or softball team you will at one time or another find yourself acting as a teacher, friend, father figure, disciplinarian, communicator, motivator and role model. Your duties will include team selection, deciding tactics, coaching, administration, collecting team fees, providing equipment, setting up the field and washing uniforms along with a myriad of other tasks. As a coach you will have already assumed most of these roles and duties, and you will have done so because you love the game.

Ninety per cent of coaching is done in practice, not in actual game situations. If practice has been designed towards specific goals, whether for a one-off game or for a whole season, then the games should take care of themselves. Obviously throughout the season problems and situations will arise that will need to be addressed by the coach as and when they occur.

Quality coaching requires several important skills and abilities. These include good communication, knowledge, preparation, dedication and consistency. Teams need direction, and it is the role of the coach to determine where the team is going, to plan accordingly and to provide the necessary leadership to reach the team's goals.

COACHING PHILOSOPHY

It is important that every coach has a philosophy, based on his views, opinions, knowledge and expectations.

Views, opinions and knowledge are based on experience, exposure to different people, books, ideas and methods. They are also based on knowledge. The good coach will want to be knowledgeable, not ignorant.

A coaching philosophy is all about the coach, how he acts, talks and behaves. To understand this philosophy it is necessary to understand the coach. What are his roles, aims, goals and motivation?

COMMUNICATION

Quality communication skills often set good coaches apart from ordinary ones. In coaching effective communication is vital. The coach needs to be able to communicate with a vast array of individuals and groups, in both formal and informal situations.

The human psyche is a complex mechanism. The baseball coach has to deal with at least a dozen of these during the course of every game and training session. All will be different, and each individual will demand the coach's attention.

He therefore has to learn to communicate with each of these individuals. Some may need coaxing and cajoling, so the coach needs to be able to talk to them in such a way to make them feel wanted. Others may need him to read the riot act to get them going.

It is important to differentiate between these types of individual. It may be counter-productive if the coach does not know the players well enough, and thus fails to communicate effectively.

'If it ain't broke, don't fix it', is a saying which is often associated with coaching and communication. However, the good coach will continually question what he says and how he says it. Constant reviewing and fine tuning will keep the coach on his toes and prevent the vehicle from breaking down.

KNOWLEDGE

A successful coach will have a thorough knowledge of the game, including techniques, skills, tactics and strategies. This will entail a lot of reading, watching, looking and learning. Knowledge can be gained from books, manuals, magazines and watching other coaches, as well as attending coaching courses, seminars and clinics.

Apart from knowing baseball, the good coach also needs to know his players, not only as players but as people. He needs to be aware of their background, needs, wants, aspirations and motivations.

This knowledge will help the coach to help each player to maximize his potential. Knowledge will help the coach to understand the players better, which will make his job easier, and on the whole more rewarding.

PHYSIOLOGY

A baseball coach needs to know how the body works, what enhances performance, and what will detract from it. The coach needs to understand physiology: speed, strength, suppleness and stamina. He needs to know what part they play in baseball, and how they can be developed to aid performance.

Fitness is a vital component of performance. The good coach will be aware of this, and structure the coaching programme to include fitness training accordingly.

TEACHING
(Fig 86)

The coach is a teacher and as such, it is vital for him to know how people learn. There are two main methods of learning: trial and error and copying. Both of these methods are based on experience. It is the responsibility of the coach to develop these learning experiences into skills and techniques.

It is important that techniques are taught in the proper sequence, and are suitable for the group being coached. A basic sequence is a follows:

1. Demonstration of the whole technique.
2. Let the players try.
3. Give feedback.
4. Break down the technique.
5. Repeat demonstration.
6. Return to full technique.

This sequence involves both trial and error and copying systems of learning.

The coach also needs to be able to analyse techniques, spot faults and correct them and offer solutions.

79

Fig 86   Coaching demonstration.

COACHING STYLE

Coaching styles vary. The good coach will change his style to suit the people and situations he is involved with. There are three main coaching styles:

1. The boss, who is an autocrat, making all decisions; the players do as they are told.
2. The minder, who operates as a minder or facilitator. He makes very few decisions and does not attempt to influence or teach his players.
3. The guider, who shares the decision-making process with the players. The guider will offer leadership and guidance, but the players will have a say.

The coach's personality will generally determine which style he will employ.

However, the good coach will realize that all these styles can help with certain groups in specific circumstances.

GAME MANAGEMENT

Before and during a game the manager has many decisions to make. These begin with the team selection and batting order. Most teams are not blessed with good batting all the way down the batting order, so the manager has to select a batting order that makes the best use of the players available.

Batting Line-Up
(Fig 87)

In general terms the batting order should follow this general format:

Lead-off   Should be a good hitter possessing a good eye, who does not swing at bad pitches and has good speed.

Second   Should have good bat control so that he can bunt, or hit and run if required. Ideally he should be left-handed so that he can pull the ball between first and second base. Should also possess good speed.

Third ⎫
Fourth ⎬ These are the strong power hitters, who will hit well, bringing in runners on base.
Fifth ⎬
Sixth ⎭

Seventh ⎫
Eighth ⎬ These will generally be the weaker batters.
Ninth ⎭

LEEDS CITY

ROYALS

BASEBALL CLUB

NATIONAL PREMIER LEAGUE CHAMPIONS 1992

UNIFORM NO.	PLAYER'S NAME	POSITION	REPLACEMENTS
3	PELLEGRIN	8	
13	MOSS	3	
9	DEWHIRST	2	
8	BROWNLIE	1	
7	LOPEZ	6	
11	REID	9	
15	SMYTH	4	
10	GOODHALL	7	
6	HOUSLEY	5	

Fig 87   Typical line-up card.

Strategy

The players available will determine the manager's offensive strategy. For example, if the team possesses no real power hitters but plenty of speed, the manager will probably operate a running offence, utilizing the bunt, steal and hit and run.

On defence the team will have worked on pre-determined defences for various situations. The main intangible is pitching: one day a pitcher may be unhittable, while on the next outing the very same pitcher may struggle. It is the manager's job to get the pitcher to concentrate and get the job done, or to change him and bring in another pitcher.

MANAGER–UMPIRE RELATIONSHIPS

Managers have a tremendous responsibility when dealing with game situations, and in particular with umpires. The conduct of the manager in these situations is a vital factor that will influence the attitude of the whole team. If the manager is loud and aggressive towards umpires, sooner or later the team will follow suit: players emulate their manager.

On-field protests are part of baseball, and it is the manager's right to protest a call. However, this should be done in a diplomatic, dignified manner. If the manager rants and raves, it will be detrimental to himself, the team, the umpire and the game. It must be remembered that everyone is involved in the game for fun, and that should determine behaviour within this context.

11
Practice Organization

Practice sessions must be meaningful for the participants, so the coach must be prepared and have pre-planned the session. The coach has to decide what he wants to teach/practice, how the session should operate, and what to emphasize. Logistically he needs to decide or know:

1. Time allocation for practice.
2. Total time available.
3. Number of players.
4. Use of equipment.
5. Equipment available.

He can then prepare a session where the players will learn, practice, train and enjoy themselves.

A standard practice session should be two to two and a half hours long. The age, skill level and dedication of the players will usually help to determine the length of practice sessions. A typical session format should include:

Conditioning	15 minutes
Team meeting	5 minutes
Warm up	15 minutes
Batting practice	30 minutes
Group drills	30 minutes
Fielding practice	15 minutes
Conditioning	10 minutes

At the start of every practice, all players should run; two laps around the field should be sufficient to warm them up.

CONDITIONING

After the warm-up is completed a routine of callisthenics followed by some gentle stretching should prepare the players for the forthcoming session. It is important that the stretching is systematic so that all parts of the body are worked. It is useful to work from the head down to the feet.

TEAM MEETING

The meeting should only last about five minutes. The coach can tell the players what the practice schedule is, which will aid the smooth running of the practice. The coach can also use this time to asses the previous game, highlighting any mistakes, for example, and stressing what needs to be worked on.

At the end of the meeting the players should do another two laps of the field before commencing warm-up throwing.

WARM-UP

The aim of the warm-up is to loosen the players' arm muscles. This should start with short gentle throws, which gradually become longer and harder.

This time can be used more productively if the players work on specific areas of their game. Pitchers can work on mechanics, infielders on quick hands and release, outfielders on longer throws.

BATTING PRACTICE

Batting practice has to be organized thoroughly so that players are not standing idle. Infielders can work on fielding and throwing skills, outfielders on positioning, and pitchers can practise their mechanics and delivery while throwing batting practice.

It is vital that the pitcher is accurate during batting practice to ensure that the hitters are seeing good pitches and are not having to chase bad ones.

The routine for batting practice should be:

1. Two bunts (one down each foul line).
2. One hit and run.
3. One hit to opposite field.
4. Five swings.

On the last swing the batter should sprint to first base and become a base runner for the next batter.

It is very easy for batting practice to become slow and boring. The coach must therefore make batting practices sharp and precise, getting the most out of the players. In thirty minutes everybody on the team should be able to bat twice.

GROUP DRILLS

Every practice should have a section devoted to group drills, where teamwork is emphasized. Both defensive and offensive strategy can be worked on. Defensive areas include bunt defence, defence against running situations (such as steal and hit and run), run downs, cut-offs and relays. Offensive areas include base running and running situations, such as bunts, hit and run and squeezes.

FIELDING PRACTICE

Every practice should include fielding drills, both for infielders and outfielders.

Outfield Drills

The outfielders should have balls hit to them at all angles, to the left, right, in front and pop flies. They should also practice throwing to second, third and home bases, hitting the cut-off where applicable.

Once the outfielders have completed their drills, they can move out to centre field and concentrate on fly balls and catching charging grounders.

Infield Drills

The infield routine should consist of ten rounds. The first three rounds will be to first, that is the coach will hit the ball to each of the infielders, who will field the ball and throw it to first base. When the ball is hit to the first baseman, he will throw to third. On the first round the ball will be hit straight to the fielders, on the second round to their right and on the third round to their left.

The next three rounds will be double plays, where the ball is hit to each infielder in turn, who will initiate the double play.

The next three rounds should be slower, where the infielders have to charge the ball, field it and throw to first base.

83

The final round is to the plate. The ball is hit to the player, who fields it and makes a throw for a force play at the plate. After catching the ball the catcher rolls another ball out. The fielder follows the initial throw, fields the second ball and again throws to the plate, this time for an imaginary tag play.

After this routine it is possible to work on particular situations, where the coach will call out the number of outs, the position of imaginary runners, the score and the inning. The coach will then hit the ball out, and the infielders will make the appropriate play.

CONDITIONING

At the end of the session every player should run. This can be done as wind sprints or base running. After the sprints the players should jog one or two laps then spend time stretching and gradually cooling down.

12
Conditioning

Both baseball and softball players need to follow a conditioning programme that develops their flexibility, strength and endurance. These areas of fitness are vital for players to maximize their ability and for the prevention of injury.

The major problems with any conditioning programme are those of time and commitment. A conditioned body needs continuous exertion. Exercise is hard work, but commitment to the exercise programme is required for any benefits to be derived.

Nevertheless, many players fail to recognize the importance of conditioning. To benefit from conditioning, the programme needs to be adhered to year round. A thorough, well-devised fitness schedule will make players stronger and faster, give them greater stamina and ultimately make them better players.

FLEXIBILITY
(Figs 88–96)

Stretching is necessary for good muscle health. Muscles need to be flexible, and for athletes they also need to be long and lean.

Baseball and softball are very stop-start sports. During a game there are many periods of inactivity, when players sit on the bench, after which they are suddenly expected to sprint, turn or slide. These are prime situations for muscle injuries. Therefore to protect the muscles, they must be in good condition.

A worthwhile stretching programme can be achieved in under ten minutes a day. Using the following guidelines, a simple stretching programme is easy to perform:

Fig 88   Shoulder stretch.

1. Warm-up before stretching.
2. Do not bounce.

3. Stretch slowly.
4. Regulate breathing.
5. Hold the stretch (10–20 seconds).
6. Stretch every day.

Exercises

1. Shoulder stretch (Fig 88). Link the fingers above your head, palms facing upwards. Push arms up and slightly back.
2. Triceps stretch (Fig 89). With the arms overhead hold the elbow of one arm and gently push the other elbow down. Change arms and repeat.
3. Front shoulder stretch (Fig 90). Place one arm straight across the body. Interlock the other arm, pulling it back towards the body. Change arms and repeat.
4. Back rotation (Fig 91). Place hand on hips and rotate sideways twisting the trunk. Do this both ways while trying to keep the hips facing forwards.
5. Trunk stretch (Fig 92). With hands by the sides, stretch down one leg. Repeat on other side. Do not bend forwards.
6. Groin stretch (Fig 93). Stand with feet wide apart, feet and knees facing forwards. Lean over one side, change side and repeat.
7. Quadriceps stretch (Fig 94). Against a wall, fence or with a partner, grab the

Fig 89 Triceps stretch.

Fig 90 Front shoulder stretch.

Fig 91 (*Top left*)   Back rotation.

Fig 92 (*Top right*)   Trunk stretch.

Fig 93 *(Left)*   Groin stretch.

right foot and pull it towards the buttocks. Repeat with the left leg.

8. Hamstrings (Fig 95). Bend one knee slightly, stretching the other leg out. Keep both heels on the ground. Push the body weight down over the bent knee, feeling the stretch in the hamstrings. Change legs and repeat.

9. Calves (Fig 96). Assume the lunge position, keeping the back heel on the ground. Change legs and repeat.

87

Fig 94 (*Top left*)   Quadriceps stretch.

Fig 95 (*Top right*)   Hamstring stretch.

Fig 96 (*Left*)   Calf stretch.

STRENGTH

Strength training has many positive effects on the overall fitness of baseball and softball players. Strength will help throwing, hitting and running as well as preventing injury.

Described below is a routine that is designed for overall strength conditioning. This programme is based on a standard weight training facility, which should be available in most sports centres.

When weight training it is necessary to adhere to the following guidelines:

1. Perform each exercise slowly and smoothly.
2. Concentrate on correct form.
3. Regulate your breathing. Exhale as you lift, inhale as you return the weight.
4. Select a weight with which you can do eight to twelve repetitions.

This routine should be completed three times a week, ideally not on successive days. Do eight to twelve repetitions of each exercise, three times. Once you can do twelve repetitions comfortably the resistance can be increased.

Exercises
(Figs 97–98)

1. Peck deck. On the peck deck machine, place each arm against the arm pads, then gently push your forearms together in front of your chest.
2. Squats. On the squat rack, place the shoulders under the pads. With the weight bend the legs until they reach a 90 degree angle. Slowly push up and repeat.
3. Calf raises. Again on the squat rack, place the shoulders under the pads. Taking the weight, raise up on the balls of your feet, then gently lower, keeping the legs straight.
4. Bench press. Lie on the bench with the legs raised off the floor, and crossed. This will keep the back straight. Push the bar up, then slowly lower it, keeping it under control.
5. Lateral pull-downs. On the lat machine, kneel or sit on the floor. Grasp the handles on the bar, pulling the bar slowly down behind the head. Slowly let the

bar up until the arms are extended, then repeat.
6. Hamstring curls. On the leg extension machine lie face down, hooking the feet under the foot pads. Slowly raise the heels to the buttocks, gently lower back down and repeat.
7. Biceps curls (Fig 97). On the curling deck, place the upper arms against the padding, isolating the forearms. Hold the bar with both hands, then raise the hands to the shoulders. Slowly lower and repeat.
8. Reverse triceps curls. Using the lat machine, hold the bar in both hands, palms facing downwards. Tucking the elbows into the waist, push the bar

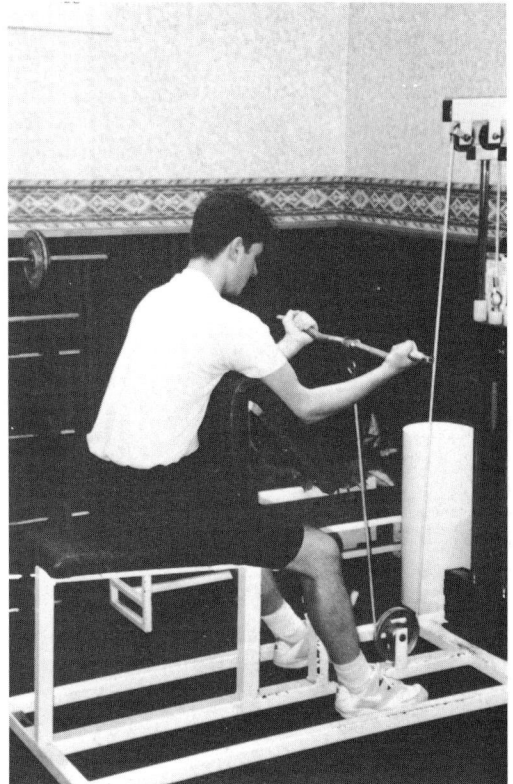

Fig 97   Biceps curls.

Fig 98   Seated press.

as far possible, then slowly let the bar go back, and repeat.

11. Quadriceps curls. On the leg extension machine, sit upright, hooking the feet under the foot pads. Raise your lower legs until they are parallel to the floor. Slowly lower, then repeat.

ENDURANCE

Endurance is as important to baseball as it is to many other sports. In most sporting activities, as fatigue sets in, technique and concentration usually begin to deteriorate. Improved endurance can delay the onset of fatigue, thereby creating a more alert and reliable player.

Endurance training can be done indoors or outdoors – outside by either running or cycling, indoors by working on a stationary bike, rowing machine or by participating in aerobics or circuit training.

To gain a training effect from this form of exercise, it is necessary to do aerobic work for at least thirty minutes, three times a week.

down until it rests on your thighs. Slowly allow the bar to come up, under control, until the forearms are parallel to the floor, then repeat.

9. Seated press (Fig 98). Position yourself on the seated press so that the bar is directly above your shoulders. Push the bar upwards, keeping your bottom on the seat. When the arms are fully extended, slowly lower the bar, then repeat.

10. Wrist curls. On the curling deck place your forearms on the pads, grasping the bar in a palm-up position. Keeping the forearms on the pads, pull upwards

THROWING ROUTINE

No conditioning programme will provide as much benefit to the throwing arm as actually throwing a baseball. Ideally players should throw every other day. The routine would begin with a warm-up session, the players only 20ft (6m) apart, playing catch.

After this warm-up phase of five to ten minutes, the players should move back to stand around 45ft (13.5m) apart and repeat the exercise. After another five to ten minutes they should move to 90ft (29m) then to 120ft (36m) apart.

The training routine should be performed by making straight, accurate throws to the partner. This is known as long toss. If performed every second day, the throwing arm will be greatly strengthened. This will in turn lead to enhanced performance and help prevent injuries.

13
Softball

EQUIPMENT

Softball bats are smaller than baseball bats. The maximum length is 34in (86cm) and the maximum diameter is 2¼in (5.5cm) with a maximum weight of 38oz (1kg). Basically the bats are thinner than their baseball equivalents.

The ball has a circumference of 11⅞–12⅛in (30cm). It weighs between 6¼ and 7oz (185g). This is bigger and heavier than a baseball.

As in baseball, all players will wear gloves. On average the gloves will be slightly larger than baseball gloves to accommodate the larger ball.

The catcher should wear the same protective equipment as in baseball. This is definitely the case with fast-pitch. Similarly, helmets are worn when batting in fast-pitch, but are not in common use in slow-pitch.

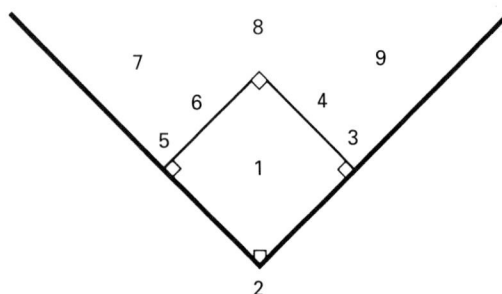

1 Pitcher	6 Shortstop
2 Catcher	7 Left field
3 First base	8 Centre field
4 Second base	9 Right field
5 Third base	

Fig 99   Standard defensive positions.

There are basically two types of softball, fast-pitch and slow-pitch. The names are derived from the way the ball is pitched.

FAST-PITCH SOFTBALL
(Figs 99–100)

Fast-pitch softball is essentially an under-arm version of baseball, with all aspects of the game (including techniques) other than pitching the same as baseball. Fast-pitch is usually played in single-sex teams, with nine players per team.

The defensive positions are essentially the same as in baseball, as is the scoring system, with the team scoring the most runs being the winners. The game is played over seven innings. A coin toss decides which team bats first.

The strike zone in fast-pitch is slightly larger than that in baseball. It extends

Fig 100   The strike zone.

from the batter's knees to the armpits, in the normal batting stance.

The other major difference to baseball lies in the rules regarding base stealing. In baseball, runners can steal bases any time the ball is in play. In fast-pitch base runners can only steal when the ball leaves the pitcher's hand in the delivery.

Playing Area
(Fig 101)

The shape of the field in fast-pitch soft-ball is the same as in baseball, but significantly smaller in size. The distance between the bases is 60ft (18.2m) as opposed to 90ft (27.5m).

For men the distance from the pitching rubber to home plate is 46ft (14m); for women it is 40ft (12m).

In softball the ball is pitched from a flat surface and not off a mound as in baseball.

HOME PLATE AREA
(Fig 102)

The pitcher's plate, home plate and bases are the same as in baseball. However, the home plate area is slightly different: the batter's boxes are longer and thinner than those found on a baseball pitch. The

93

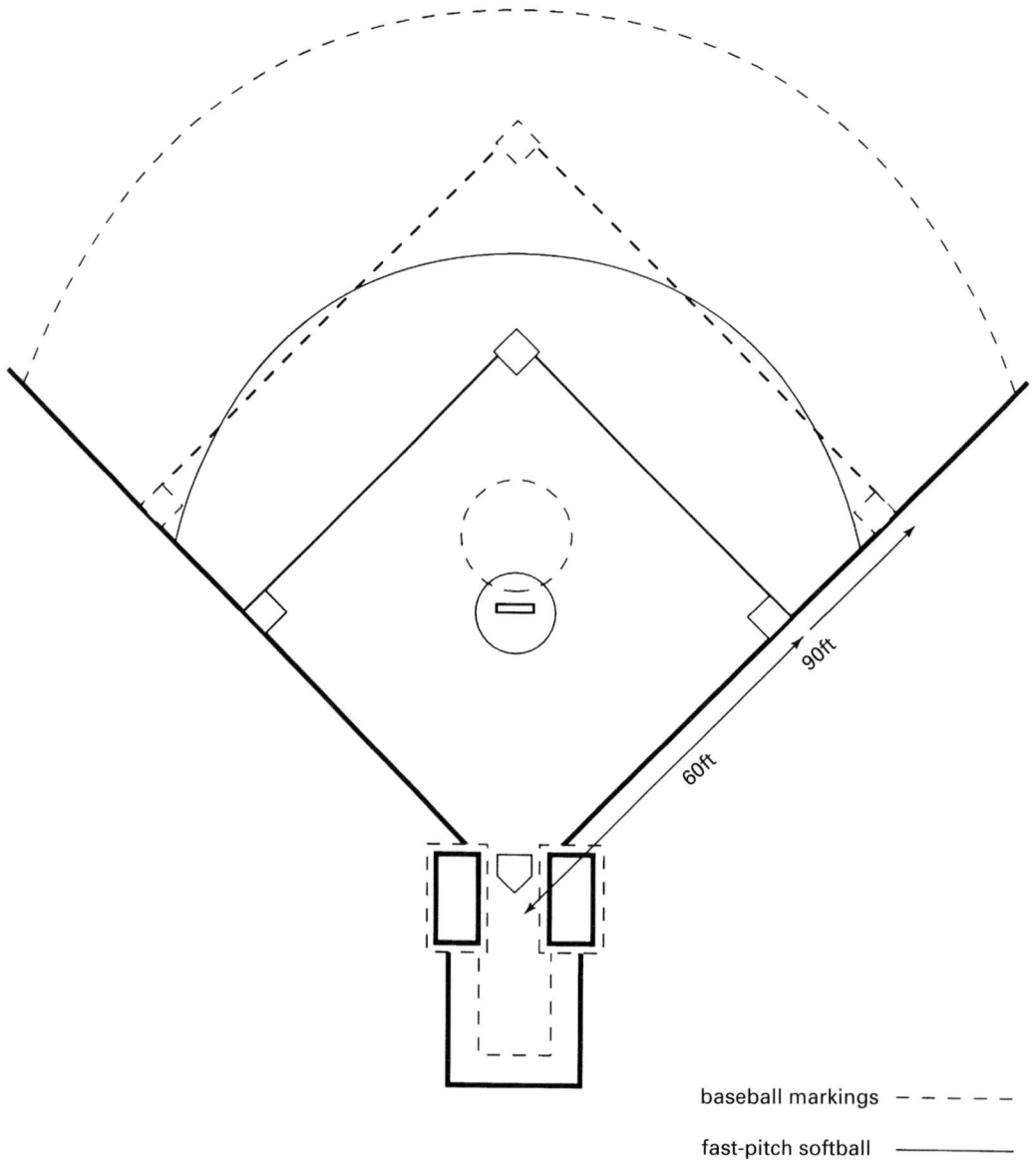

Fig 101   The playing area, compared to baseball.

baseball markings — — — — —

fast-pitch softball ——————

60ft

90ft

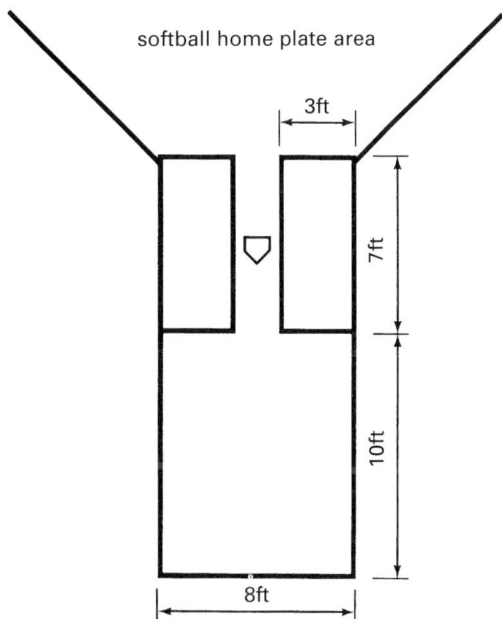

softball home plate area

3ft

7ft

10ft

8ft

Fig 102   The home plate area.

pitcher must come to a complete stop, with his shoulders in line with first and third base. The ball must be held in both hands, in front of the body. This position must be held for at least one second, but not for more than ten seconds.

The ball is held at waist level directly in front of the body. Both feet must be in contact with the pitcher's plate, but they should be in a position from which forward momentum can be obtained.

The right-handed pitcher should stand with the heel of the right foot on the front edge of the plate, the toe of the left foot on the back edge. The feet should be

catcher's box is much larger than its baseball counterpart.

Pitching

There are several stages to the pitching motion. They are:

1. Presentation.
2. Grip.
3. Wind up.
4. Release.
5. Follow through.

PRESENTATION
(Fig 103)
Before a pitch can be delivered, the ball must be presented to the batter. The

Fig 103   The presentation position.

95

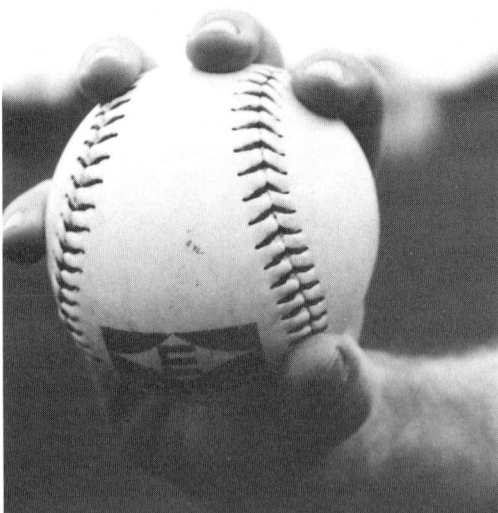

Fig 104   The fastball.

slightly less than shoulder width apart. This will be the other way round for a left-handed pitcher. This puts the pitcher into a comfortable, efficient position from where the ball can be delivered.

GRIP
(Figs 104–106)
The grips for the standard pitches are essentially the same as for the baseball pitches discussed in Chapter 3. They include a fastball, curveball and a knuckleball.

Delivery

The delivery stage includes the wind up, release and the follow through. There are two basic deliveries for softball pitching, the windmill and the slingshot.

Fig 105   The curveball.

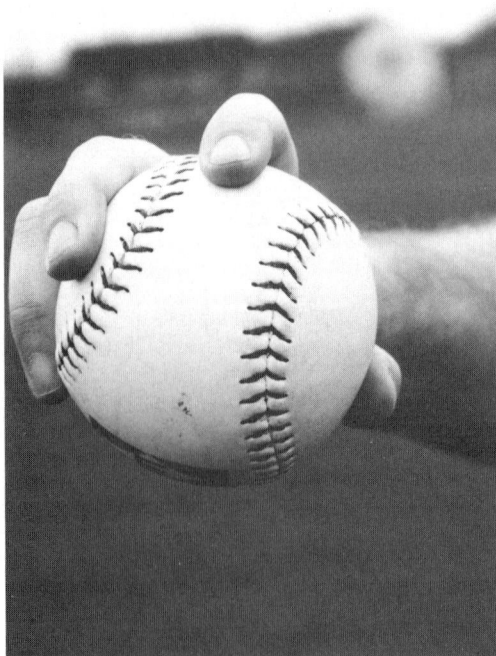

Fig 106   The knuckleball.

WINDMILL

(Figs 107–113)

From the presentation position the right-handed pitcher's weight should be moved onto the right foot, as both hands descend to the right side of the body (left side for left-handers).

The delivery arm is slightly bent and swings forwards and upwards. The unweighted heel lifts off the ground, and the unweighted foot strides directly towards home plate. The other foot acts as a pivot, pushing the body forwards, with the arm swinging back and down to complete a full 360-degree range of motion.

As the back foot leaves the pitching plate, the ball should be released. The point of release will vary from pitcher to pitcher, and is also dependent upon the pitch selected.

Fig 107   The windmill delivery (1): presentation position.

Fig 108   The windmill delivery (2): the wind up stage, with both hands moving upwards to initiate the pitching motion.

Fig 109   The windmill delivery (3): the wind up stage, with the pitching arm at the vertical.

97

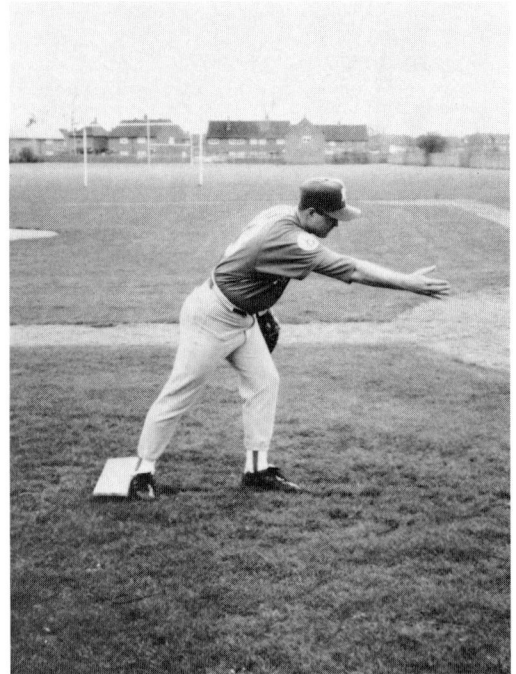

Fig 110 *(Top left)* The windmill delivery (4): side-on view as the pitching arm begins its downward path.

Fig 111 *(Top right)* The windmill delivery (5): the pitching arm in forward motion, preparing for release.

Fig 112 *(Bottom left)* The windmill delivery (6): the pitching arm at release point, eyes fixed on target.

Fig 113 *(Bottom right)* The windmill delivery (7): the release position.

After the ball is released the drive leg steps through, and the pitching arm continues upwards on the follow through. The pitcher should then assume a fielding position as quickly as possible.

SLINGSHOT
(Figs 114–119)
From the presentation position, the body will rock backwards, shifting the body weight onto the right foot for right-handers. The pitching arm swings downwards and backwards.

From this position the weighted foot drives the body forwards, the unweighted leg strides towards home plate, and the pitching arm swings down and forward directly towards the target.

As with the windmill, the release will vary from pitcher to pitcher. However, the ball is generally released in front of the pitcher's body, and the follow through should bring the pitcher into a fielding position.

Fig 114 The slingshot delivery (1): presentation position.

Fig 115 The slingshot delivery (2): the wind up stage, with both hands moving upwards.

99

Fig 116   The slingshot delivery (3): the
pitching arm at its furthest extension,
preparing for the downward path.

Fig 117   The slingshot delivery (4):
the pitching arm on its downward
path, going into the release position.

Fig 118   The slingshot delivery (5):
release point.

Fig 119   The slingshot delivery (6):
the ball is released and the pitcher is
ready to follow through.

All the other fundamental skills, including throwing, catching, infielding, outfielding, batting and bunting are the same as in baseball. Fast-pitch also uses the same tactics and strategies as are used in the parent game.

SLOW-PITCH SOFTBALL
(Fig 120)

Whereas baseball and fast-pitch softball are games dominated by pitching, slow-pitch softball is essentially a hitting game. It is played by single-sex and mixed teams, although in Britain the mixed variation of the game is more popular.

Unlike baseball and fast-pitch, in slow-pitch there are ten players per team. The extra fielder plays in the outfield, and is called a rover.

The scoring system is exactly the same as in baseball and fast-pitch. A run is scored each time a player completes a circuit of the bases, touching each base in turn.

As in fast-pitch the game is played over seven innings, with a coin toss deciding which team bats first.

The strike zone in slow-pitch baseball is larger than that in fast-pitch. It extends from the knees to the highest point of the shoulder, in the batter's normal batting stance.

Fig 120   The slow-pitch strike zone.

Balls and strikes are called in the same way but in slow-pitch the batter is out if the third strike is fouled off.

Playing Area

The shape of the field is the same as for both baseball and fast-pitch, but the infield area is slightly larger than the fast-pitch infield. The distance between the bases is 65ft (20m) and the distance from the pitching plate to home plate is 46ft (14m). This is the case for male, female and mixed teams. The home plate area is exactly the same as that in fast-pitch.

The equipment used is the same as in fast-pitch.

Stealing

Unlike in baseball and fast-pitch, stealing is not allowed in slow-pitch. Base runners must stay in contact with the base until the ball reaches the plate, or is hit by the batter. If the ball is not hit all runners must return to base. If a runner fails to keep in contact with the base he will be called out.

Pitching
(Fig 121)

Pitching in slow-pitch softball is a relatively easy skill which the majority of players can master.

In slow-pitch the fielding team must assume every batter is going to hit the ball. It is the pitcher's job to force the batter to hit the ball in a certain way, ideally ground balls or fly balls, which give the fielders the opportunity to make the appropriate plays.

The pitch must travel in an arc between 6ft and 12ft (1.8–3.6m). This obviously prevents the pitcher delivering the ball too fast, as it would then not be able to travel in the specific arc.

Pitching Sequence

There are five phases to slow pitching:

1. Presentation.
2. Wind up.
3. Stride.
4. Release.
5. Follow through.

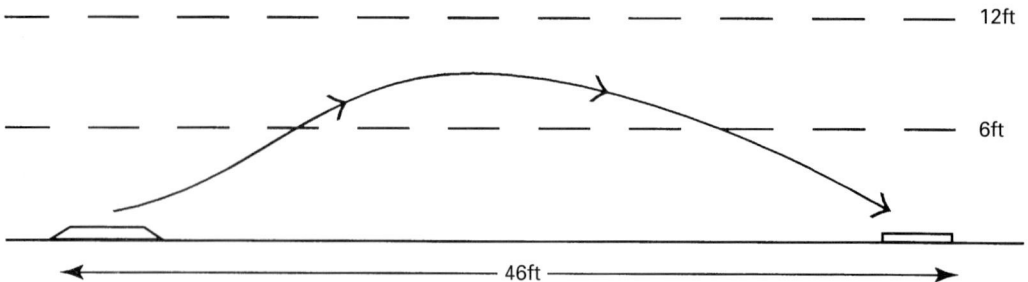

Fig 121   Pitching trajectory.

Fig 122   The presentation position.

STRIDE
(Fig 124)
As the arm reaches the top of its backwards arc, the pitcher steps forwards with the pivot foot (left foot for a right-hander, right foot for a left-hander). Simultaneously the pitching arm moves downwards and forwards, with the fingers behind the ball.

RELEASE
(Fig 125)
The ball should be released in front of the body with the fingers under the ball.

FOLLOW THROUGH
(Fig 126)
After the ball is pitched, the pitcher needs to get into a good fielding position. The back foot comes forwards bringing the pitcher into a square-on position. The

PRESENTATION
(Fig 122)
The pivot foot needs to be in a comfortable position, remaining in contact with the rubber. The ball is held with a standard three-fingered grip, ready to pitch. The weight should be on the back foot.

WIND UP
(Fig 123)
In the first phase of the delivery, the pitcher's weight shifts from the back foot onto the pivot foot. As this is happening the pitching arm moves downwards and backwards in a winding up motion.

Fig 123   The wind up.

Fig 124   The stride.

Fig 125   The release.

knees should be bent, with the hands in the ready position.

PITCHING LOCATIONS
(Figs 127–129)
Successful pitchers will be able to pitch to different locations using the whole width of the plate. The location of the pitches will usually depend upon the position of the batter in the batter's box.

With the large strike zone available, the pitcher can pitch deep, short or medium pitches. Ideally this will pose the batter different problems and limit his hitting power.

Fig 126   The follow through into the fielding position.

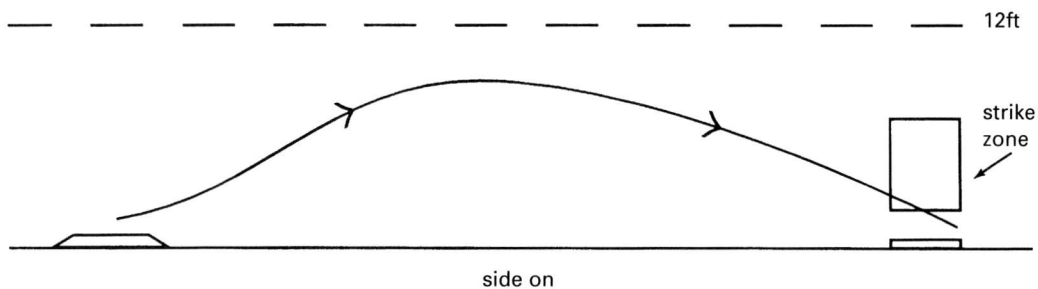

12ft

strike
zone

side on

Fig 127 Short-pitch location.

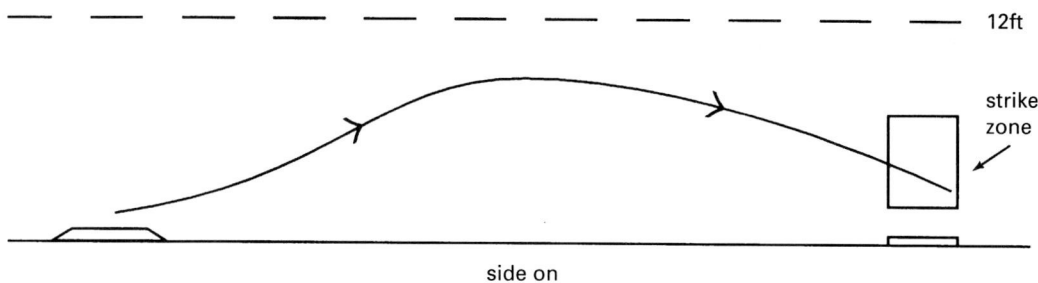

12ft

strike
zone

side on

Fig 128 Medium-pitch location.

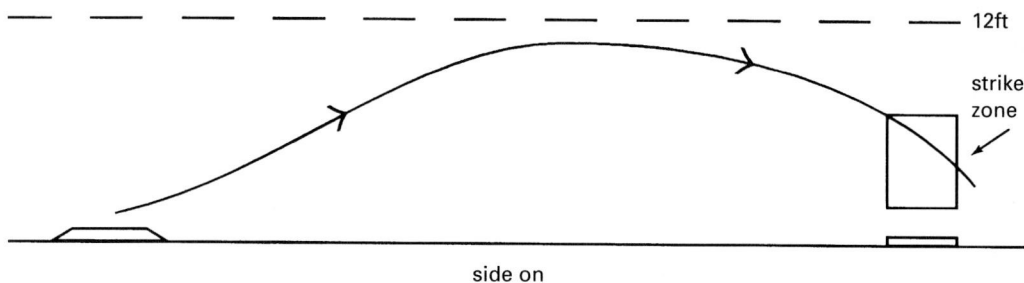

12ft

strike
zone

side on

Fig 129 Deep-pitch location.

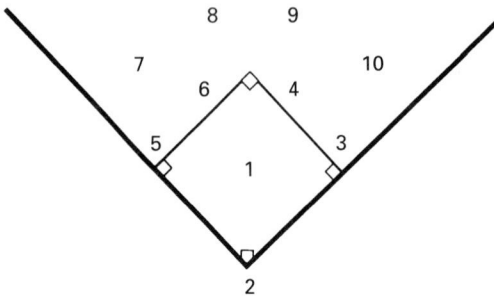

1 Pitcher   6 Shortstop
2 Catcher   7 Left field
3 First base   8 Left-centre field
4 Second base   9 Right-centre field
5 Third base   10 Right field

Fig 130 Team defence with four outfielders.

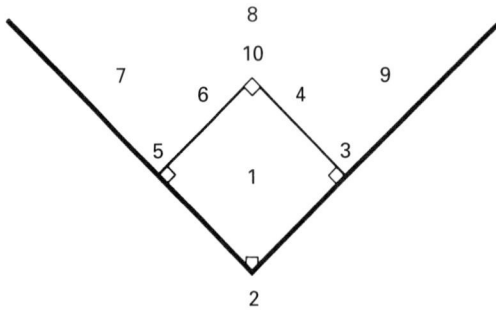

1 Pitcher   6 Shortstop
2 Catcher   7 Left field
3 First base   8 Centre field
4 Second base   9 Right field
5 Third base   10 Rover

Fig 131 Team defence with three outfielders and a rover.

Team Defence
(Figs 130 & 131)

There are two basic alignments for soft pitch: four outfielders, or three outfielders and a short outfielder (rover).
Positions
1. Pitcher – the most important player on the team. Must have an accurate throwing arm, be a good fielder and be able to lead the team.
2. Catcher – possibly the poorest fielder on the team. Does not have too many fielding opportunities. Good position for a left-hander.
3. First base – again a good position for a left-hander. Must be a good fielder; does not need to have a strong arm.
4. Second base – usually the second best infielder after the shortstop. Must be athletic and have a good range to be a good, solid fielder.
5. Third base – does not have to be as agile as a shortstop or second baseman, as there is less area to cover at third. Must be quick and brave as a lot of hard-hit balls go to third. Needs to have a reasonable arm.
6. Shortstop – this is the most difficult position to play, so the shortstop is usually the best fielder on the team. Needs a strong arm, good range and safe hands.
7. Left fielder – this is the most important outfielder, as most right-handed batters will hit the ball to the left field. Needs to be fast and have a strong arm.
8. Centre fielder – needs to possess similar qualities to the left fielder, although is probably not as good a fielder.
9. Right fielder – often the team's poorest fielder. Most right-handers do not hit to right field very often, so it makes sense to place a poorer fielder in right field.

10. Rover – again, usually a poorer fielder, who can be hidden.

Batting

In slow-pitch every player is a hitter. In most circumstances even the poorest players on the team will be able to hit the ball. As is the case with baseball and fast-pitch it is important that batters do not swing at bad pitches. When the ball is a strike it is important to hit the ball where it is pitched; that is, if it is on the inside part of the plate the ball should be hit to the left field.

The batter must take a full swing at the ball: in slow-pitch, bunting and chopping the ball are illegal tactics.

Glossary

Assist A throw to a team mate enabling him to make a put out.

Balk An illegal action by the pitcher with a runner on base. As punishment all the runners advance one base.

Ball A pitch that does not enter the strike zone, and is not swung at by the batter.

Base A base is sited at each corner of the diamond, 90ft apart. They are first base, second base, third base, and home.

Base hit Ball hit into fair territory enabling the runner to reach base safely. The ball is not mis-fielded.

Base on balls If the pitcher throws four pitches outside the strike zone, and the batter does not swing, the batter is entitled to a free walk to first base. (Also called a walk.)

Bases loaded First, second and third base are all occupied by runners.

Batter's box The area where the batter must stand when batting.

Battery The combination of the pitcher and catcher.

Batting average The batter's average is calculated by the number of hits divided by the number of times at bat.

Bench The area of the field where the teams sit. Also called the dug-out.

Bottom The second half of any inning.

Breaking ball Any pitch that deviates in flight, such as a curveball, slider or knuckleball.

Bull pen Area of the field where pitchers warm up.

Bunt When the batter allows the ball to hit the bat rather than swinging at it, creating a soft hit to the infield.

Catch When the fielder catches the ball in the air without it touching the ground.

Catcher The player who fields directly behind the batter.

Catcher's box Area where the catcher must stay until the pitcher delivers the ball.

Catcher's interference Where the catcher impedes the batter. The batter is awarded first base.

Change up A slower pitch, usually thrown with the same motion as a fastball to deceive the batter.

Choke up To hold the bat further up the handle.

Count The number of balls and strikes the batter has received.

Curveball A breaking ball that curves in flight.

Cut-off A player who receives a throw from the outfield.

Dead ball When the ball is out of play.

Designated hitter A batter who hits instead of the pitcher.

Double A two-base hit.

Double header Where two games are played on the same day.
Double play A play in which two players are put out.

Error A fielding mistake that would have put a runner out.

Fair ball A ball that is hit into fair territory.
Fair territory The area of the field between first and third baselines.
Fastball A pitch thrown as fast as possible.
Fly ball A ball that is hit into the air.
Force play When a fielder retires a runner by touching the base.
Foul ball A ball that does not go into fair territory.
Foul territory The part of the field that is outside the first and third base lines.
Foul trip A batted ball that goes sharply backwards and is caught by the catcher.

Grand slam When a batter hits a home run with the bases loaded.
Ground ball A ball that is hit along the ground.
Ground rules Rules that make allowances for any field obstructions.

Hit When a batter reaches base after hitting successfully.
Home run When a batter hits the ball and completes a circuit touching all the bases in one go without stopping.

Infielder A player who plays in the infield.
Inning When both teams have batted once, an inning is complete.

Knuckleball A speciality pitch that deviates in flight.

Line drive A hard-hit ball that travels directly on a line.

Middle infielders Collective name for second baseman and shortstop, who is also called the pivot.

No hitter When no base hits are conceded by a pitcher throughout an entire game.

On deck circle Where the next batter waits for his turn to bat.
Out Where the batting team have a player out. The team is allowed three outs per inning.

Passed ball Where the catcher fails to field a pitch that should have been controlled, and runners advance.
Pick off To catch a runner off base.
Pinch hitter A substitute batter.
Pinch runner A substitute runner.
Pitch A ball delivered by the pitcher to the batter.
Pitch out A pitch deliberately thrown wide of the plate, to help the catcher throw out base stealers.
Pop fly A ball that is hit high into the air and is caught by an infielder.
Power alleys The space between the outfielders.
Put out When a fielder retires an offensive player.

Relief pitcher A substitute pitcher.
Run A run is scored when a runner touches all the bases in the correct order.
Run down When a runner is caught between bases.
Runner An offensive player who is on or running towards any base.

Screwball A speciality pitch.

Single A successful hit that enables the batter to reach first base.

Slider A pitch that breaks at the last minute.

Split-fingered fastball A fastball that dips at the last minute. (Also called a forkball).

Steal Runners can attempt to reach the next base whenever the ball is in play. This is called stealing.

Strike A strike is a legal pitch if: (i) the batter swings and misses; (ii) the ball passes through the strike zone; (iii) the ball is hit into foul territory (this only counts for the first two strikes); (iv) the ball hits the batter in the strike zone.

Strike out When the batter has three strikes.

Strike zone The area over home plate between the batter's knees and armpits.

Suicide Squeeze When a runner is on third base, he will sprint for home as the pitcher delivers the ball. The batter's job is to bunt the ball into play. If he does the runner will score, if he fails the runner will be out.

Switch Hitter A batter that can bat both right-handed and left-handed.

Tag When a fielder touches a base runner while holding the ball.

Tag up When a fly ball is hit with less than two outs, runners must tag the base they were on, after the ball is caught before they can advance.

Top The first half of an inning.

Triple Where a batter reaches third base safely on one hit.

Wild pitch A pitch that is thrown so inaccurately that the catcher cannot field it.

Useful Addresses

British Baseball Federation
66 Belvedere Road
Hessle
North Humberside
HU13 9JJ

National Softball Federation
81 The Dome
Dome Way
Redhill
Surrey
RH1 1DJ

Major League Baseball
350 Park Avenue
New York
NY 10022
USA

**American Baseball Coaches
Association**
PO Box 9665
North Amherst
Massachusetts 01059-9665
USA

National Coaching Foundation
114 Cardigan Road
Headingley
Leeds
LS6 3BJ

Index